FOCUS

Five Critical Areas of Spiritual Growth for Christians and Churches

Jay McCaig

DEDICATION

This book is dedicated to my wife, Vee, who thinks I am better than I am and to the Holy Spirit who makes me better than I am.

CONTENTS

PREFACE

As a Pastor I spend much of my time praying and meditating over what to preach. It was during one of these times of prayer that I asked God to show me the areas that myself and our congregation should be focused upon, and He gave me the message of this book. What started out as a prayer turned into a sermon series, and now a book that can be shared around the world. And since this book started as a series of sermons it reads in a distinctively conversational tone.

The acrostic **FOCUS** stands for Freedom, Others, Cross, Understanding & Salvation. What you will find in this book:

FREEDOM – What is true freedom and how is it obtained? Freedom is one of those words that has been overused and diluted so much that most students today would have a hard time defining what it really means. God gives us a freedom beyond anything ever penned by any leader, poet, or philosopher; a freedom that is beyond our comprehension but readily available to you today. Freedom from your addictions. Freedom from those who hold you back. Freedom from the forces of evil. Freedom from yourself.

OTHERS – One of the greatest distinctions of the Christian faith is the mandate from our Lord to reach out to the world in love on His behalf. Not just to those like us or near us, but a mandate to take His Word to every person. While this task may seem overwhelming or even impossible, it becomes possible and even achievable when we follow the simple, clear directions

He has given us.

The CROSS – Everything changed at the cross of Calvary, from the way we worship to our payment for sin. The way God relates with us and the way that we relate with Him. Are you still living like those from before the cross, or are you living in the newness of that new relationship? What happened at the cross has made available to you a new power and freedom, the likes of which the world can't even imagine.

UNDERSTANDING – You have a God that not only knows you better than any other but desires you to know and understand Him. He has already given you everything you need to not only know Him, but to also live an abundant life while you are here on this earth. Learn how to understand His Word and why it is so important to do so.

SALVATION – You will make lots of decisions in your life, decisions about where to live, what to drive, who to marry and where to work. Many you will get right, and many you will get wrong. But there is only one decision that you will make that will mean the difference between Heaven and hell. Even if you have a history of making bad decisions, get this one right and your eternity will be secure.

It is my prayer that this book will be as much of a blessing to you as it has been to me. Please pray for me as I pray for you. Also, if you are ever in the Central Florida area, I want you to visit Crossroads Baptist Church and tell say "Hi". You can get directions and all of the info you need at *www.LifeAtTheCrossroads.com*.

How to use this book

Pray before you start and ask the Holy Spirit to guide you as you explore this book. Each of the five chapters is designed to be a stand-alone work, so you can start wherever you feel led and go from there.

At the end of each chapter you will find two sections; one titled **"Let's Go Deeper"** and the other **"For Pastors"**.

The **"Let's Go Deeper"** section will help you take what you have just studied and apply it to your life. Take your time answering the questions and completing the tasks. I would be thrilled to hear how each section has impacted your life, so please email me at Pastor@LifeAtTheCrossroads.com and tell me your story.

In **"For Pastors"** I have included thoughts and tips for preaching the contents of each chapter to your congregation. Feel free to use whatever touches your heart and is profitable to the ministry God has given you. Please send me an email and let me know the results you experience, at *Pastor@LifeAtTheCrossroads.com*. Pray for me as I pray for you!

Jay McCaig

CHAPTER 1 - FOCUS ON FREEDOM

The F in FOCUS is for Freedom. Freedom is something that I find very, very interesting, partly because it is a concept that is so misunderstood today. If we were to go down to the local Wal-Mart and start asking people, "Do you understand freedom?" most would be hard-pressed to give a proper definition. We should have a unique perception of freedom here in the United States. We experience or have experienced in this country a level of freedom that most of the world have never seen. Most of the world can't even comprehend the freedoms that we have in this country. That's why it may seem shocking to you, mind boggling to you that, whenever we go into a country, liberate that country and we set up freedom, and we set up a democratic government, that within 5-10 years, they have elected back into power the very dictators that they were screaming for freedom from. They don't know how to live in freedom, because they have never experienced true freedom; they have no concept of it. If you have never lived in freedom, freedom can be scary and you may end up reverting right back into that familiar

1

bondage.

We are blessed in this country, because not only do we experience freedom, but many of us were born in a free country. Freedom is really all that we know; unfortunately, freedom is also something that is slowly leaving us. It is something that we have grown so accustomed to that we have forgotten how valuable freedom is and are willing to sacrifice freedom in this country for safety, for comfort, or a cell phone. We are ready to sacrifice our freedoms and it hurts to watch, knowing how many people have given their lives so that we could have freedom. We are just willing to say, well here, take them away. My freedom is more important than my safety, my freedom is more important than having my road paved, my freedom is more important than my refrigerator. I really, really worry about this country. I worry about the direction that we are headed in. Some of you are old enough to remember when things were vastly different. Things weren't perfect; things have never been perfect in the United States. We won't even kid ourselves that things were perfect at one time. Things weren't perfect, but the freedoms that we enjoyed were much, much greater.

As I write this we are preparing to observe Martin Luther King Day in our community. There are a lot of varied opinions out there about Martin Luther King, Jr. Unfortunately today, too many special interest groups, too many fake "reverends" have taken his message and perverted it into something that it isn't even close to his message; but like him or hate him, one of the things that Martin Luther King was good at, was public speaking. He knew what freedom was and he knew what freedom wasn't. When I talk about Martin Luther King people remember his speeches, one in particular. Remember his famous "I Have a Dream" speech? I want to share with you the ending of that speech, because he talks about freedom in such eloquent words, better than I ever could. On August 8, 1963, his speech ended in these words:

"Let Freedom reign from the prestigious hilltops of New Hampshire. Let freedom ring from the mighty mountains of New York. Let freedom ring from the heightened Alleghenies of Pennsylvania. Let freedom ring from the snowcapped Rockies of Colorado. Let freedom ring from the curvaceous slopes of California. Not only that, but let freedom ring from Stone Mountain Georgia. Let freedom ring from Lookout Mountain Tennessee. Let freedom ring from every hill and molehill of Mississippi from every mountainside. Let freedom ring and when this happens, when we allow freedom to ring from every village and every hamlet in every state, in every city, we will be able to speed up that day when all God's children, black men and white men, Jews, Gentiles, Protestants, and Catholics will be able to join hands and sing in the words of the old negro spiritual, free at last, free at last, thank God almighty, we are free at last."

That's powerful. When I first started preaching, another pastor told me, "If you want to learn how to speak, if you want to learn how to preach with power, watch Martin Luther King. Watch how he carries himself." And so I did. My style is nothing like his, but I hope to one day speak with such power. When you watch him, you lose yourself in his words, because they were powerful and because he understood freedom. If you go to Washington DC, Philadelphia, Boston, or many other places in this country, you will see hundreds of different memorials for people who have fought for this freedom and who have died for this freedom. As great as the freedom is in this country, the greatest freedom in the world, this freedom pales in comparison to the freedom that you enjoy as a Christian. Do you know that you have a freedom that is beyond what Martin Luther King talked about? You have a freedom beyond what any soldier ever died for. You have a freedom that is beyond all that. You have a freedom that is bought and paid for by the blood of Jesus Christ. You have that freedom.

In Ephesians 1:7 – 10 it says, *"In whom we have redemption through his blood, the forgiveness of sins, according to the riches of his grace; Wherein he hath abounded toward us in all wisdom and prudence; Having made known unto us the mystery of his will, according to his good pleasure which he hath purposed in himself: That in the dispensation of the fulness of times he might gather together in one all things in Christ, both which are in heaven, and which are on earth; even in him"*.

The key word in this passage is the word "redemption." Unfortunately it is a word that we don't use very much anymore and even when we do use it, we are talking about coupons or something minor; we are not using it in the proper term, but that word redemption is an important word. It is a difficult word to understand because it is difficult to understand all that the redemption of Jesus Christ means. It is a difficult word to put into earthly terms. The closest that I could think of in that word redemption, is the picture of the pawnshop. When you take something to a pawnshop, you take your property, you give it to them and they give you a price that is much, much less than the value of what you are giving them. The item that you give them is still yours, but you have no control over it anymore. The item that you give them is still yours, but you can't use it anymore. Until that day, when you are able to go back in and bring them the redeeming price then that thing that was yours the whole time, but was kept from you, that was not able to be expressed as yours, now that thing has been redeemed; now it is yours, now it can live and be used to its fullest potential. That's redemption.

The word redemption literally means to be loosed, to be free, or be delivered by the payment of a price. When we are redeemed we have been let loose. When we are redeemed, we have been set free. It is not just an opening of the door; there is a price that has been paid for us to be redeemed. That price is the shed blood of Jesus Christ. We have been bought with a price. We have been redeemed by a price; we are not redeemed for nothing. We are not redeemed just to be redeemed; we are redeemed by a price. In these verses we read, Paul declares that price, the price and the purpose of redemption. We are going to look at that in just a moment, but first I want to back up just a bit and consider the questions; why do we need to be redeemed? What is the purpose of this redemption? Jesus answered that in John chapter 8. He answered that when he was teaching in the temple. In John 8: 31, he answers that question for us on why we need to be redeemed.

John 8:31 – 36 says, ***"Then said Jesus to those Jews which believed on him, If ye continue in my word, then are ye my disciples indeed; And ye shall know*** *the truth, and the truth shall make you free. They answered him, We be Abraham's seed, and were never in bondage to any man: how sayest thou, Ye shall be made free? Jesus answered them, Verily, verily, I say unto you, whosoever committeth sin is the servant of sin. And the servant abideth not in the house for ever: but the Son abideth ever. If the Son therefore shall make you free, ye shall be free indeed."*

Look at that middle part again, *"Whosoever committeth sin is the servant of sin."*

Maybe you've heard people say something like, "It's just a little sin, it is not like I am out killing people." *"Whosoever committeth sin is the servant of sin."* It doesn't matter if it is a big sin, it doesn't matter if it is a little sin; you are still a servant to that sin. *"And the servant abideth not in the house for ever: but the Son abideth ever. If the Son therefore shall make you free, ye shall be free indeed."* Do you see the picture of the pawnshop? When you sin, you are taken away from the father's house. You are taken out of his grasp and you become a servant to sin. You still belong to him, but he can't use you now, he does not have access to you now; you have been set aside. You have set yourself aside. You have become a servant of sin, instead of a servant of God. Get the picture?

I want you to understand freedom and how valuable it is, and yet Jesus Christ has given it to us. Jesus did not use the word redemption in John 8, but his words certainly reflect that. The Bible is clear that when we are born of this world, we are born as sinners. As soon as you and I are able to make a conscience choice we choose to sin and because we consciously choose to sin, it makes us servants of sin, but there is a redemption.

In order to become a part of God's family, I have to be set free from my sins. I have to be, say it with me, redeemed. We need to be redeemed. We have to be redeemed.

You see, there is this misconception in this world that we're all God's children. Haven't you heard that before? "Why can't we all get along, aren't we all God's children?" The Bible says no, we are not all God's children. That should be eye opening for you today. We are born children of this world, not children of God. John chapter 1, tells us about how redemption can transform us into the children of God. John 1:12 says, ***"But as many as received him, to them gave he power to become the sons of God"***. The only way you can become something is if you were not it in the first place. For example, a woman cannot be given the power to become a woman, because she is already a woman. We can't become something that we already are. The only way we can become sons of God, is if we were not already born the sons of God. Becoming the sons of God is part of that redeeming. When we are redeemed, when we are paid for, when we are bought, when that price is accepted, that is when we become the children of God. The great thing is that even though none of us are born the children of God, all of us can become the children of God. Every single one of us; it doesn't matter how good you think you are, it doesn't matter how bad you think you are. You can be redeemed into the family of God. It is your choice, to be redeemed or not.

The only way that we can be redeemed, is that a price has to be paid. If my soul is in hock in a spiritual pawnshop, the only way I can get my soul out is that a price has to be paid. It is a price that I cannot pay for myself, because I am the one that's in hock; I can't pay for my own soul to get out, and nobody else can pay to get my soul out, because they are in the same situation that I am. I have asked people before, when you die, are you going to go to heaven? And they say, "Oh I hope so." That is one of the most heart-wrenching statements I have ever heard anyone say. To hope I am going to heaven; to hope. If you are hoping to go to heaven, you are not going to heaven. Hope won't get you to heaven. The Bible says that you can know, not hope that you are going to heaven! When someone says "I hope," what they usually mean is that they hope when they get to heaven, and there is going to be a big scale up there, they are going to put all their good stuff on one side and all their bad stuff on the other side and if there is a little more good than bad, then they get to sneak into heaven. That is not the way it works. You see, there is not enough good that we can do, to ever offset the bad that we have already done. It is not possible, because while we live on this earth, even after we have been saved, we still continue to sin. Hopefully you do not sin as much as before you were redeemed. Hopefully it distresses you when you sin, after you have been saved. Hopefully it is much more difficult, but it is going to happen. That is the reality of it, and it happens to all of us. As we continue to sin, we continue to add onto it. It is like paying off a credit card and only paying the minimum each month. The interest rate keeps on building up and building up and we can never get ahead of it; it just keeps building and building and we need somebody else to pay our debt. Somebody who has no debt that needs to be paid has to pay our debt, and that is where Jesus Christ comes in. Jesus Christ had no debt to pay, because he had no sin. Jesus had no debt to pay, so he was able to pay our debt. In our text, in Ephesians 1:7 it says, *"In whom we have redemption through his blood"*. What is the price of redemption? The price is the shed blood of Jesus Christ. There is nothing else that will pay our debt. That is it. That is the price of redemption; there is nothing else that can be given. There is nothing else that can be presented. It is that one thing.

In 1 Peter, the author writes about our redemption as well; 1 Peter 1:18-19 *"Forasmuch as ye know that ye were not redeemed with corruptible things, as silver and gold, from your vain conversation received by tradition from your fathers; But with the precious blood of Christ, as of a lamb without blemish and without spot."* The only way, the only possible way that our sins can be forgiven and we can be set free from the slavery of sin, is through the shed blood of Jesus Christ. Anything else is not sufficient. Peter even says that even things like gold, silver, and church tradition are not enough. Why? Because they are corruptible, they are not forever, and it is not a permanent payment. There is one permanent payment and that is the blood of Jesus Christ.

Sin is one of those things that always presents itself as being something pleasurable and before you know it, we are locked up by it. We are shackled by it, we are chained by it and we look around and we say, how did I get here? Some of you who used to listen to Paul Harvey on the radio, you can still listen to the reruns of his show on many stations. He gave an example one time of how an Eskimo catches and kills a wolf. When a wolf would come around, it would devastate an area. So the wolf would have to be eliminated, but the problem with wolves is that they are violent and they are actually difficult to kill. So the Eskimo would take a knife, a very sharp knife and they would dip it in animal blood, and they would let it freeze. After it froze, they would stick it in more animal blood and they would let it freeze. They would continue this process until it was encased in animal blood and then they would take it to a place where a wolf was known to travel and they would stick it in the snow with the blade up. Before long, the wolf would smell the blood and he would be drawn to that knife. When the wolf found that knife, he would taste the blood, he would lick the blood. As he licked the blood and the blood started to melt in his mouth, he would lick it more and more fervently, until the blood that he was licking up was his own blood as his mouth was being torn to shards on that knife. Sin; it starts out as looking tasty, and it starts out as looking like something we want. Then, with every lick, it becomes more and more devastating, more and more damaging, until finally it destroys us. You see, Satan's plan for you isn't to control you. Satan's plan isn't to occupy you, Satan's plan isn't just to derail you from God's plan, Satan's plan is always the same; he wants you destroyed. He will be satisfied with nothing less. He wants you destroyed. Satan hates you. Why? Because God loves you, God loves you and for that very reason,

Satan hates you.

What of this process of redemption? This process of redemption, according to Ephesians, is *"according to the riches of his grace; Wherein he hath abounded toward us in all wisdom and prudence."* The process of redemption is God's grace. That's how we get redemption; there is nothing that we can do to earn redemption. We have to get it through God's grace. What is God's grace? God's grace is getting something that you don't deserve. Grace is something that is difficult for us to understand sometimes.

I liked teaching in the jail because the inmates understood grace, because they understood where they were in life. They understood what their situation was. They understood whatever it was they were being charged with. They understood that they were going to stand before a judge and that judge was going to give them a sentence and, if their defense attorney had done their job, then they already knew before they walked in what their sentence was going to be. The law has sentencing guidelines, so if this was their third DUI, they knew going in what was the most or least they would be sentenced to. They knew going in, they were going to get something between those two extremes. You get caught with drugs, this is what you are going to get. You slap your grandma, this is what you are going to get. Whatever the crime is, there is a sentencing guideline and they understand that, but whenever the inmate stands before a judge, what he hopes and prays for is grace. What does grace look like in a courtroom? Your sentencing guidelines say you should get between 1-5 years but you know that the judge can change those sentencing guidelines for certain situations. So even though you are told that you are going to get between 1 and 5 years, you stand before the judge and you hope that you get 6 months or time served, or probation, something much less than what you deserve and sometimes the earthly judges will give that to you. But because an earthly judge is a corruptible judge and he gives out corruptible grace, he doesn't give out perfect grace. The Bible says that what you deserve as sinners, you deserve death, but because of God's grace, even though the sentencing guideline says you deserve the death penalty, you get something much less. Since your judge is the perfect judge, you get perfect grace. You don't just get a reduced sentence; you get no sentence at all. Your sentence is gone. Instead of death, you get life, then even more grace; you get eternal life, that's grace! Grace is the unmerited favor of God.

Grace is something that is poured out upon us every day. I don't believe that we recognize God's grace as much as we should. We don't consider that everything put into our hand is put there by the grace of God. Everything that we do is enabled to us by the grace of God. The fact that you are in this world today is because of the grace of God. We have a building, chairs to sit in, air conditioning, and food on the table, because of the grace of God. Everything we have is because of God's grace. He pours his grace out upon us to the point that it is overwhelming to us. When we start listing the stuff that he has done for us and is doing for us, it becomes overwhelming. I used to play football, so my mind usually either goes back to sports analogies or food. Grace to me would be to be able to eat whatever you want at a buffet and still lose weight. That doesn't work. In football though, when I picture grace, do you know what I see? You've all seen it. If you have ever watched a football game at the end, you have seen this happen. They win a big game, everybody is pumped up, they are excited and the coach is over on the sidelines and pretty soon you see a couple of guys sneak up behind him and what do they have? The Gatorade or bucket of ice water. And while he is not paying attention, what do they do? They pour it over his head. It is overwhelming. I just love the looks some of these coaches give. They should be expecting it, but they never are. As Christians, shouldn't we be expecting God's grace? Yet, we still get surprised by it. The Coach should be expecting it, but he is overwhelmed by it, because it isn't just a cup of water, it is gallons and gallons and gallons more of Gatorade or water and ice than he knows what to do with. It overwhelms him—that is the picture of grace. When God pours his grace out upon us, it seems to come out of nowhere and just overwhelms us. That is the redemption process.

God's grace is the process by which he makes redemption possible for his children. So, what is the purpose? The purpose is very simple. The purpose of redemption is restoration. Back in Ephesian's God said, *"Having made known unto us the mystery of his will, according to his good pleasure which he hath purposed in himself: That in the dispensation of the fulness of times he might gather together in one all things in Christ, both which are in heaven, and which are on earth; even in him."* Jesus restores us from sin, when we accept him. That is the purpose of the Cross, to restore us. See, when God created this world, he created a perfect world; he created a world without sin. His plan is of the restoration of that perfect world. When he brings us back home, his plan is to take us to a place where there is no pain, there is no trouble, and there is no death, because there is no sin. There is complete restoration, complete redemption. That's what we look forward to. That's what we are redeemed to.

I mentioned earlier that we continue to sin sometimes after we have been redeemed from sin, after we have been saved from sin. The Bible talks about sin as being bondage and our freedom through that redemption is the removal of that bondage. I want to give you a picture of what sin looks like.

Picture two people standing with their wrists tightly secured in handcuffs.

The first person is wearing strong, metal handcuffs, the kind your local police officer might use. As difficult as it may be this person can move around and accomplish things just like an unshackled person. They can go about their life, they can eat, they can drink, and they can do just about anything they would normally do. They look the same, the only difference is they are shackled. So everything that they do is going to take more effort, it is going to be harder, and some things they will never be able to get done. This is how the world lives without Christ. They live without the freedom of redemption. They live a life less than the life God had planned for them.

Now, what happens when they get redeemed? They get redeemed and the handcuffs come off. Now they are free, they can do anything that they need to do.

They have the ability to work unencumbered, because now they have been completely freed from the bondage of sin.

Here is an odd thing that Christians do, though. Before they didn't have a choice; they were born into sin, they were born shackled. Remember before, I said that sometimes we will go into a country, give them democracy and they don't know how to act. Before long, they are back into the same type of thing that happened beforehand. It isn't different with Christians, you see; as Christians we can get right back into that same sin, but there is a difference this time. This time, we were not born into it. This time we choose to sin, so the bondage is different.

Now picture a different person tightly secured in cheap, plastic handcuffs. The bondage is different because the bondage is a willful bondage, it is a weak bondage, and it is not even a real bondage. It is toy bondage, it is a fake bondage, but so many Christians live like this. They live like they are in bondage, but in reality they are in a bondage that has already been broken, that they have already been freed from. That bondage can't hold them, unless they choose to be held by it. See, there is the power of redemption. The power of redemption is the fact that we have to choose to be put back into bondage. We can never be put into real bondage again.

You see the difference between the Christian and the world? The difference between the saved and the unsaved? The unsaved is in bondage, and there is nothing that they can do about it except be redeemed by the Blood of Christ. The Christian, on the other hand, chooses the bondage and it's not even a real bondage, it is a chosen bondage.

Too often Christians have their little pet sins. Sins that they were once in bondage to before Christ and now they choose to again be a servant to. Maybe your pet sin is that carton of cigarettes sitting on your counter, maybe it is the beer in the refrigerator, maybe it is the food in the refrigerator, maybe it's the pills, maybe it's the TV, maybe it's an uncontrolled tongue; whatever your pet sin is, you know it. You are thinking about it right now. Whatever that thing is, whatever that sin in your life is that you are choosing to be a servant to, you are choosing to be in bondage to it. When you are about to partake I want you to do this: pray to the Father, in the name of Jesus, through the power of the Holy Spirit; I want you to pray that God will set you free from that bondage. That's it. I don't ever want to see you being a slave to sin again. Jesus died to free you from sin. It is kind of... rude isn't really a good enough word- it is kind of ungrateful. When Jesus Christ sacrificed everything to free us from sin, for us just to rush back in and put the bondage back on is hateful.

Christ died so that you can be freed from sin, to live the fullest life possible through Him on this Earth and one day to be with Him in eternity. Never settle for anything less in your life.

Let's Go Deeper

1. What does true freedom mean to you?

2. Write down your account of when you were redeemed by Jesus Christ.

3. Share an example of God's Grace upon your life.

4. What sin have you allowed to place you back into bondage since you were redeemed?

5. Will you pray now and ask God to remove that sin from your life?

6. Write Ephesians 1:7 in the space below and make plans to memorize it this week.

For Pastors

First of all, I want to thank you for taking the time to read this book. I know how busy you are and how valuable your time is. When teaching Freedom in our service, we had two volunteers come up on stage to illustrate the difference between the actual bondage to sin an unsaved person experiences as opposed to the willful bondage to sin that the Christian faces. We handcuffed both volunteers. For the volunteer portraying the unsaved person we used real, police style handcuffs and on the other volunteer we used children's plastic cuffs. If you have a police officer in your congregation they may be willing to administer the cuffs. (Don't forget the key.) After they were both secure, I talked through how the one in the real cuffs is subject to them and there nothing short of being freed by another, Christ, would remove their bondage. On the other hand, the one who willfully sinned could easily break free from the grip of sin because he already had the power of Christ within to set him free. I had the volunteer pull apart his hands to illustrate how easily sin can be defeated by the Christian who relies upon Christ. At the end of the service I had more volunteers stand by the exit and give each person a pair of child's handcuff to take home and display somewhere where they would be reminded how weak sin is when they live in Christ.

Jay McCaig

CHAPTER 2 – FOCUS ON OTHERS

I was looking at famous last words on the internet this week. Those last requests or comments made by people before they died. We put a lot of emphasis on the last words, the last thing that someone says. Often in those final words we get a picture of what that person finds truly important. Some of those famous last words that struck me were:

The Italian artist, Raphael, simply said "happy" before he closed his eyes.

Blues Singer Bessie Smith's last words were, "I'm going, but I'm going in the name of the Lord."

The great inventor and artist Leonardo da Vinci stated, "I have offended God and mankind, because my work did not reach the quality it should have."

Author, Sir Arthur Conan Doyle, turned to his wife and said, "You are wonderful."

Percy Grainger, an Australian composer, his dying words were to his wife - he said, "You're the only one I like."

John Wayne died at age 72 in Los Angeles. Near the end of his life he was getting a little bit of dementia. His wife had come in, and she asked him, "Do you know who I am?" And he looked at her and he said, "Of course I know who you are, you're my girl, I love you." And then he died.

I have thought about this myself, and I have tried to come up with something good to say whenever I get to that point in my life; I want to have something really cool to say, so people talk about it later. I haven't come up with anything, yet. I'm having a feeling that my last words will be silly like, "Pass me another doughnut." Then I'll stand in glory, and be like, "Really? That's what I said right before I left. Pass me a donut." That was it, those are my last words? That was it. So I'm still looking.

But last words are important. I want to take a moment and look at the last words of Jesus Christ. The last words that Jesus spoke to us before he ascended. These last words are found in Acts 1:6-9 *"When they therefore were come together, they asked of him, saying, Lord, wilt thou at this time restore again the kingdom to Israel? And he said unto them, it is not for you to know the times or the seasons, which the Father hath put in his own power. But ye shall receive power, after that the Holy Ghost is come upon you: and ye shall be witnesses unto me both in Jerusalem, and in all Judaea, and in Samaria, and unto the uttermost part of the earth. And when he had spoken these things, while they beheld, he was taken up; and a cloud received him out of their sight."* Those are Jesus' last words. This is the emphasis that he wanted to make to us. He wanted us to do something, He wanted us to go someplace, He wanted us to understand something.

What did He mean by Jerusalem, Judea, and Samaria? Jerusalem was their home town, where they lived and worked, and the people that were already around them. What is Judea? Judea encompasses Jerusalem, but then much, much more – we would liken it to a state, province or maybe a county. Samaria is a separate area altogether; a neighboring area, but a completely different area. And then the uttermost, the uttermost refers to everywhere else.

So what is He trying to tell them? First of all, He's telling them, you need to take it to your people. You need to take it to your neighbors; you need to take it to the people around you, and the people they work with. But they needed to think bigger than that. They needed to expand it past their city; they needed to expand into the next city, and into the next city. They needed to expand it into their county, state or the region that they were in. Basically those areas and those people that would be within a day's journey of them. But they weren't to stop there, they were to take it to the next people group. You know what the big difference was between Judea and Samaria? Gentiles. There weren't very many gentiles in Jerusalem. There weren't a lot of gentiles in Jerusalem, but Samaria had a mix of Jews and gentiles. This was a big command, one that many probably scoffed at. Typically the Jewish people looked down upon the Samaritans, believing them to be beneath the Jews and unworthy of their time or respect.

Then take it to the uttermost. Take it to people that are different than they are. Take it to people that were raised differently. Take it to people that look different. Take it to people that talk different. They had a different language. Take it to Judea, take it to Samaria, and then take it to the uttermost. You know where the uttermost is? It's everywhere. Everywhere that there's people, they were told to take the gospel to everyone, everywhere. This created a new concern for the Jewish believers; it meant taking The Gospel to the pagans, into areas of the world that were violent and unhospitable.

This command changes very little for us. The command to us isn't specifically about Jerusalem anymore; it's not specifically about Judea, it's not specifically about Samaria, but that command still applies to us today. Our Jerusalem is our home town. The people around us, our families, our co-workers, and our neighbors. These are the people Jesus commanded us to reach with His last words. Our Judea could be our extended sphere of influence or for the church, it could mean expanding their geographical outreach.

And then he wants us to get really crazy, and he wants us to take it to a whole new place, our Samaria. That's not just expanding out, that's expanding into a whole different place. Different cultures, different people. People who, even though similar to us, are still different enough from us to take us out of our comfort zone. Different racial groups, different economic groups, people with struggles different from our struggles. Maybe this is manifested by reaching out to the homeless, the widows and the fatherless. Or maybe it is reaching out to our politicians, doctors and instructors. This could be a people group living in your area that has a different language or culture.

But then he said the uttermost; the uttermost is beyond Samaria. It's to the rest of the world; it's to wherever there are people. He's talking about people who haven't heard the word of God. He's talking about people who are worshiping something other than the one true God. He's talking about people who do things completely differently that live in completely different, strange, unusual worlds. That's where he's telling us to take His Word.

The uttermost also includes those cultures that would deny and persecute Christ. There are places in this world where it is illegal to be a Christian. There are places in this world where they cut the heads off of Christians in the name of their god. Those are the uttermost; those are the people we're supposed to reach. It's every creature, not just the ones that like us. 2 Timothy 4:2 tells us *"Preach the word; be instant in season, out of season; reprove, rebuke, exhort with all longsuffering and doctrine."* You know what the difference is between preaching in season and out of season? In season is the preaching that takes place in the church house. It's easy because people come expecting to be preached to. You go to the church house to worship God. I don't think there's anybody, at least I hope there's not anybody that goes to Church, sits down in the pew and says, "Whoa whoa whoa, we're going to sing songs and hear from the Bible, really? That's not what I signed up for, that's not what I'm here for." No, preaching in the church is in season, it is expected, it's easy.

What is out of season? Out of season is preaching when and where it is not well received. The extreme out of season would be those Christians that - right before they got their heads cut off - proclaimed their Jesus. It would be Paul standing before King Agrippa in his bonds, and King Agrippa saying in Acts 26:1 *"Thou art permitted to speak for thyself."* And Paul taking the opportunity to tell the King about Jesus and the effect His love had brought in his own life rather than to beg for forgiveness. That's preaching out of season. Because King Agrippa didn't want to hear it. The people in the room didn't want to hear it. That's out of season. Out of season is when we preach or we proclaim the word of God, when it's not comfortable, when it's not convenient. In places that are strange to us, to people that are strange to us. I guess it's not politically correct to say, "People are strange," right? Well, people are strange to us, and we're strange to them. But they still need the gospel. Because it doesn't matter how strange we find somebody. It doesn't matter how undesirable we find somebody, they still need the gospel. Think about the most undesirable people group to you, or the most undesirable type of person you can think of - Jesus died for that person. That soul is valuable to him. We can't get caught up in all of our petty prejudices; we can't get caught up in the "me first" culture of this world. We have to understand, what Jesus' last words for us were to go and tell everybody. Not just the easy ones, not just the convenient ones, but to tell everybody.

So how are we going to do this? How are we going to tell everybody? We, as Christians and Ambassadors of Christ, are responsible for the entire world. Do you know that? This command went to us. So we need to have a plan in place; we can't afford to become stagnant. We can't afford to become comfortable. We can't afford to do the same thing every week and interact with the same people every week. We can't afford that, and the earth can't afford that. Christ died for something bigger than that. And if all we're going to do as a Church body is just sit in a room and sing songs and listen to the Pastor preach every Sunday, we're wasting our time. We may as well sell the property and split the money up, because we're just wasting time. Because the task that God has given us is so much bigger; it's so much greater.

So how are we going to do this? How are we going to reach our town? Well, the most obvious way is through the local, Bible teaching Church that God has planted in your community. God gave us the local Church so that we can come together and we can get mobilized and we can go out, and we can reach our communities for Him. The Church does this by teaching people how to tell people about Jesus. Training them to be effective soul winners and sending them out into the community. The Church was given for your benefit and blessings, to magnify your efforts and reach your community. If you are not part of a local, Bible teaching Church you must find one as soon as possible. Christians were not meant to live separate from other believers; we are meant to come together to Worship and serve Jesus. It is through the local church that you will most effectively reach your

Jerusalem.

Unfortunately finding a good church is not as easy as it once was. Satan is the great counterfeiter and he has created many counterfeit churches in your community. Look for a Church that preaches and teaches the death, burial and resurrection of Jesus. Look for churches that condemn sin while loving the person, as Jesus did. Look for a Pastor who does not censure God's Word to avoid conflict. Avoid churches whose goal it is to entertain for the sake of filling seats or padding their bank accounts. Church shouldn't be boring; after all, Worship is a celebration, but a church's purpose should not be to entertain. Jesus' true Church is concerned over the soul that is lost and on their way to Hell above all else. If you need help email me, and I will do my best help you find a Bible teaching, Christ centered church in your area: *Pastor@LifeAtTheCrossroads.com*.

How do we reach our Judea? Judea isn't just another physical place; it's an expansion of our physical sphere of influence. It's reaching into people groups that aren't being reached. How do we do that? Sadly, the local Church has become one of the most segregated places in our community. To change that we must create ministries that reach out to people who are different from us or who are struggling with different problems than us. Things like Jail Ministries, Hearing Impaired Ministries, and Foreign Language Ministries are easy ways to get started reaching your Judea.

An Internet ministry is a great way to reach not only the shut-ins in your community but also to take the Gospel to places where there are no Bible teaching, Christ centered Churches. Most of what is being passed off on TV and the internet today as Worship is paganism, led by apostates. We need more Bible believing Churches represented in that arena. A strong internet ministry impacts not only your Judea but also your Samaria and the uttermost. Keep in mind though that an internet ministry is always second best to the local church. The church is a called out, gathering body; not a bunch of individuals sitting on their couches watching online.

But what about when you have to be home due to sickness or mobility issues? Most of the choices that are out there on TV right now are not good. There are a lot of false Pagan doctrines being taught. Use the same standards used to pick your local church when picking an internet or TV Ministry. Look for a ministry that helps people to worship Jesus Christ. A ministry that draws them in and makes that connection with Christ better than it has been before. And the ideal way, and the very, very best way is to come together is by gathering. That's what the church is, a local called out body of believers. We're to come together, this is biblical, but there are people that cannot be called out. They cannot physically gather together for whatever reason. That is where the Internet Ministry is a great asset. God has given us the wisdom to make great strides in technology so that we can use it to bring honor and glory to Him.

At Crossroads Baptist Church, we are in the infancy of developing our internet ministries. As of this writing, one of our more popular resources is the audio recordings of our sermons. Through our audio teachings we have seen people accept Christ as their Saviour and lead a fuller, more productive Christian life. Recently we were contacted by a group of Christians living in Pakistan who are using the audios not only for weekly studies but also to practice their English language skills. But that goes beyond our Judea doesn't it? Now we're getting to the uttermost, and we are getting ahead of ourselves.

How do we reach our Samaria? The very best way to reach Samaria is by planting churches. There is not another method that even comes close in its effectiveness to reaching the lost than planting new churches. The number of Bible believing & teaching churches in America is not even close to meeting the need. Most experts agree we need at least one Bible believing church for every 10,000 people in a region. So in a county the size of Osceola County, FL, where I reside, there are about 300,000 people So to meet the need in Osceola County we need at least 30 bible believing & teaching churches. Not churches that are teaching man's doctrine, not churches that are teaching a doctrine that's been tainted, where they add something to Grace of God for salvation. But a pure teaching grace of the gospel. We need 30 in Osceola County. I know of six. Maybe I missed a few, maybe some smaller churches that I'm not familiar with, but it it's definitely less than 10. We should have 30, and we have 6. We have counties all across the United States that have zero Bible believing churches. 9 counties in Florida have zero Bible teaching churches. They have churches, but they're not preaching the gospel of Jesus Christ, or they're preaching the gospel and that it takes more than Jesus Christ to be saved. Does that shock you? That should shock you. You know why that is? Because we're not starting churches. We are too busy worrying about what happens within our little groups that we don't notice that there are millions dying without Christ because of us. We need to be starting churches. We need to be training up leaders that are going to carry the gospel out of our local churches and into other places, into our Samaria.

There is a right way and a wrong way to start a church. Sometimes you can tell by the name of a church how they got their start. I saw a new church the other day called Greater Freedom Church; it was one block down from Freedom Baptist Church. Chances are that the "greater" church was the result of a church split. Churches should not be started by splits. Churches should be started in love, not through hate and bitterness. Men should not start churches; real churches are started by other churches. Churches birth churches. It's the only way they can start. Jesus Christ is the head of the church, so for a man to separate himself from the church and start a new church, he is separating himself from Christ to start the church. Churches start churches. Most of the churches in my community weren't started by other churches; they were started by men. So some of the biggest churches I know were started because somebody was sitting there saying, "I can do this better. I have a better way." And they left without the blessing of the church, and without Christ's blessing, and they went out and they started their own church.

That's not how churches are supposed to be birthed. Churches aren't supposed to be birthed out of anger. Churches are birthed out of love. That's why when Crossroads Baptist Church came to St. Cloud, we came as a mission work out of Winter Haven Baptist Church. Winter Haven Baptist has started several churches around the state. They get it; they understand that the best way to reach our Samaria is by starting churches. All Bible believing churches need to be starting churches. To start churches we need to be training up leaders. To help meet that need, we will be starting a Bible institute here at Crossroads Baptist Church this year. This Bible institute won't be just for church planting, though. It'll be a Bible institute that anybody who wants to can come and learn more about the Bible.

Here's one of the big statistics about planting churches. Whenever a church is planted, almost 80% of the people that join that church were not churched anywhere. Most of them weren't even saved. And they accept Christ, and they join the church. For an established church, most of the people that join the church are people that have left another church. So we're really not growing the body of Christ, we're just kind of moving people around a little bit.

That's huge. Planting churches is still the number 1 way to reach the lost in the United States and in every country, its planting churches that helps us fulfill our Samaria.

In America the reality of it is that if someone has to travel more than 30 minutes to get to church, they're not going to church. Now that's wrong, I understand that. In other countries, people travel for hours to get to a good church. But that's not the mindset here in the United States. People desire instant gratification. It's not uncommon for people in large cities, like New York, to be born, live and die and never leave their Borough. They never even get to the other side of the city. They stay right in Queens, or they stay right in Brooklyn; that's what they know, that's where they stay. We need to start churches in every Borough, in every county, every city, and every neighborhood. The good news is, is that not only one church has this burden or this duty. Our Lord is leading churches all across the World with the same passion.

One of the simplest ways to start a church out of your church is to begin looking at the demographics of your church. Do you have 10 – 15 people from a neighboring town attending your services? That may be the baby church that God is incubating right under your nose. Pray that Jesus will lead a man to step up and lead this fledgling group. When budget time comes around, start setting aside money for whatever opportunity God may present to start a new church. Birthing a church is scary stuff. Some of you may be thinking, "Wow, do we really want to give up a chunk of our congregation for that?" Yeah, oh yeah you do. An amazing thing happens when a church sends people out to start a new church; the old church grows! Every church that I've ever seen that sends groups of people away to start churches gains more in numbers than the people they're sending away. Why? Because God blesses those that follow his will. It's as simple as that.

If you want to grow as a church, you have to reach your Jerusalem, you have to reach your Judea, you have to reach your Samaria, and you have to reach the uttermost. So how do we reach the uttermost? We reach the uttermost by supporting missionaries who do basically the same thing as a church planter. I don't support missionaries that just go out to live the "missionary life", and neither should you. Missionaries should be church planters. Men and women who go and start churches, train up local Pastors to take that church over and lead that church and then go and start another church. They do this over and over. This method has worked so successfully that there are now more Bible believing churches sending missionaries out of the Philippines, then there are missionaries being sent out of the United States. We reach the uttermost by sending, praying for, and financially supporting Missionaries.

At Crossroads Baptist Church we fund our missionaries through a faith promise approach, where above and beyond our tithes, we make a promise to God and say, "God, how much do you want me to give to support our missionaries?" Whether it's $5 a week or $10 a week. And it may be money that you don't even have, yet, but you say, "God I'm going to, above my tithes. I want to give to missions; I want to reach the uttermost. And God, if you provide it, then I'll give it." It's called a faith promise. It's not looking at your bank account and saying, "Okay, this is how much I can afford." It's putting your bank statement away and saying, "God, how much do you want me to give?" And then, "God if you want me to give $10 or you want me to give $20 or if you want me to give $40 a week - whatever it is you want me to give, then God you've got to give it to me. You've got to provide it, because if you don't provide it, I can't afford it." It's called a faith promise. That's how we fund our missionaries.

We also gather with other churches. We gather with other Bible believing churches from around the country, and we put our funds together. We have a clearing house in Springfield, IL overseen by the Baptist Bible Fellowship. We use this clearing house because they do not charge a fee or take a percentage out for administrative fees. What that means is that if we want to send $100 to one of our missionaries in Guatemala or one of our missionaries in Mexico, or one of our missionaries in China we send $100 to the Mission Office, designated for a particular Missionary and every dollar goes right into the hand of the missionary so that it can be used for the work of God in that country. We partner with other churches so that every month that missionary gets funding.

We also take mission trips. We go into these countries and we share the gospel with them and we serve the people as we serve God. We meet the immediate need, whether that is food, water, clothing, medical care, etc. and we also meet their eternal Spiritual need of a Saviour. But we also go there because it's an encouragement for us. It's good for us to go and see the need worldwide. It helps us put into perspective how much God has blessed us here in America. I know that Missions is not as popular in the churches as it once was. As we have become more self-centered it has been harder for us to acknowledge the needs around the world. We need to start seeing the world through the eyes of God; God loves the World. He tells us this in His Word - John 3:16 *"For God so loved the world, that he gave his only begotten Son, that whosoever believeth in him should not perish, but have everlasting life."*

Now your focus may be more in one area, because if one person's focus is more on Jerusalem and another's is on Judea, and another's is on Samaria, and another's is on the uttermost. Then as a church body, we're reaching all of them. But for someone to say, "Well I'm all about Jerusalem and the rest of you - I'm not giving anything for any of that." Or, "I'm not helping with that, I'm not supporting that." That's the old self talking, that's not Christ. Christ says we reach all. The first church had this problem. The church, the people that Jesus specifically gave His order to. Do you know what they did when he left? They said, "That sounds great Jesus, but we're just going to worry about Jerusalem." And that's what they did. And they built a huge church in Jerusalem. Thousands coming to know the Lord. One of the most successful churches in all of history, but they didn't do what God said. They didn't take His story to the whole World.

Acts chapter 8 gives us a glimpse of what will happen if we continue to ignore the need for Christ around the World. I want you to see the results of people only worrying about their Jerusalem. This is what'll happen to us if we only worry about people in our immediate sphere, if we only worry about us and ours. And by the way, if you're going to do that, if you're going to have that worldly mindset - which by the way is a satanic mindset - if you're going to have that satanic mindset and say, "I'm only worrying about Jerusalem," don't take it to the next step; don't infect your evilness upon other people. Don't go to others who want to go on a mission trip, or people who want to give to missions, or those who want to help start a church in another city.

Acts chapter number 8. Verse number 1. It says:

"And Saul was consenting unto his death. And at that time there was a great persecution against the church which was at Jerusalem; and they were all scattered abroad throughout the regions of Judaea and Samaria, except the apostles."

You see what happens when we don't do what God says? They didn't do what God says. When they stepped outside of God's will they stepped into the attacks of Satan. And through their persecution God's Will was still done. They went to Judaea and Samaria.

Acts 8:2-3 *"And devout men carried Stephen to his burial, and made great lamentation over him. As for Saul, he made havock of the church, entering into every house, and haling men and women committed them to prison."*

Sadly, though, many good men and women died or were imprisoned. And God used Saul to disperse the church.

Verse number 4 & 5; *"Therefore they that were scattered abroad went every where preaching the word. Then Philip went down to the city of Samaria, and preached Christ unto them."*

Phillip was a great man of God. But he wasn't doing what God told him to do. God told Phillip, "You go to Samaria." Phillip said, "I'm going to stay in Jerusalem." The whole church said they were going to stay in Jerusalem. The whole church said, "Hey, we're going to worry about our town, and we're going to worry about our people, and we're not going to worry about those people on the other side of the world. We're not going to worry about those people in the next town, or the next county, we are just going to sit here in our comfortable pew and let someone else worry about that." And God dropped a bomb in the middle of the church and dispersed the Church of Jerusalem against their will. He told them, "Now, you're going." And that's when Philip went. And he spoke, he preached the gospel to Samaria and people believed, people were healed, a man was set free from witchcraft, and great Joy flooded the city!

The church is being persecuted in the United States today more than I've ever seen the church persecuted in my lifetime. And we can point fingers at the politicians, we can point fingers at the Liberals, we can point fingers at the abortionists, we can point fingers at the atheists. We can point fingers at everybody we want, but do you know why the church is being persecuted today in the United States? Because we're not doing what we're supposed to do. And when we don't do what we're supposed to do, God allows persecution. To disperse us and move us. You know why the church in China is growing so fast? Because God is allowing them to be persecuted. My prayer is that we can get back to what we used to do. We can get back to what the church used to do in this country, reaching our Judea, reaching our Samaria, reaching our uttermost, and doing what God said to do. So then not only will he grow us here, but his Church will grow around this world and we can avoid that persecution. I don't know about you, but I don't like to be persecuted, I don't want to see people imprisoned; I don't want to see Christians imprisoned for their beliefs. We're very close to that.

I met with a Pastor last week. He has a church in Oklahoma and he had a judge issue a court order against him from preaching parts of the Bible - in the United States. The judge says, "You cannot preach this chapter and you cannot preach this chapter." It was all about the homosexual movement. He says, "You cannot use the word homosexual, you cannot use the word gay, you cannot use the word lesbian. In the pulpit or in your personal life, you are not allowed to use these parts of the Bible in America." And he says, "That's illegal." But the judge did it. And it took him over 2 years and $10,000 in legal fees to have another court look at that and say to the first judge, "You can't do that." And so it's gone, for now, but it took 2 years for him to reclaim that right. Every time he spoke on the banned subject - and by the way it made him preach about it a lot more. But every time he did it, he was fined. Every time he spoke and read from Romans chapter number 1, he was fined. They placed liens against the church; they were getting ready to take the church property when this other judge finally stepped in.

You may be saying, "Well that's illegal, this is the United States." And you are correct, that's why it was overturned after 2 years and over $10,000. $10,000 by the way, they don't get back. That's money that's all been spent by attorneys and court fees. This is what we're facing in United States. I don't want to face persecution. I'm not going to avoid it, I'm not going to stop because of it. But the way that we can avoid it, the right way to avoid it is not to back down, but to be even bolder and more vocal, and start doing exactly what Jesus Christ told us to do. If the church in Jerusalem had done that, and they had gone, they wouldn't have been persecuted.

39

Perhaps Steven wouldn't have died, that day, if they'd done what they were supposed to do, but they didn't.

The church is made up of individuals; I am not the church. I'm just the loud mouth of the church God has given to me to be His under-shepherd in. We all have different parts. We're all the body, and it takes each one of us doing our part. It takes each one of us finding our place, our ministry. It takes each piece working together to make all of this work. I can't reach St. Cloud by myself, much less our Judea, Samaria, the uttermost - I can't do that by myself. I haven't even been able to reach my neighborhood. I can't reach everybody, and neither can you. That's why God gave us a body. That's why we come together. But it takes each person doing their part. You need to find your ministry, find your point of service. If you've never accepted Christ as your savior, you're not even part of the body yet. If you've accepted Christ as your savior, then find your place. Find your ministry. Maybe your ministry is to teach Sunday school. Maybe your ministry is to lead music, or maybe your ministry is to preach. Maybe there's another loud mouth in here; we can use another mouth. Maybe your ministry is the foreign mission field. Maybe God's been calling you to a country and you've been putting him off, putting him off, and putting him off. Maybe it's not to go to another land, maybe it's not for a long term mission, maybe he's just calling you for a short term mission. Maybe God's telling you, "Serve right here in Jerusalem."

You know those people I talked about before that only want to deal with Jerusalem and forget the rest of the world? We had that problem here at Crossroads

Baptist. Last summer we had a person who made vocal their feelings about us taking a mission trip to Guatemala to a couple of other people in the church. They were saying things like, "Why are we worried about those kids in Guatemala? What about our kids here? Let's worry about our kids here first, and then we'll worry about those kids in Guatemala, those different kids." And they started planting that seed throughout the church. And it got back to me. I didn't say anything to them, because the people they were talking to were wise enough to understand and see it for what it was. Instead, we prayed for that person. So then at Christmas time we were taking up collections for the kids here in Osceola County, the kids that we were, according to this person, supposed to be taking care of first. And I watched. I didn't say anything but I watched. Do you know how many presents they brought? None, not one. When given the opportunity to reach out to the kids here in their Jerusalem they chose to ignore them as well. You see, they don't really care about anyone but themselves, they were just using their fake indignation over the mission trip as a smoke screen for the real problem. Their mind and their heart is still a mind and a heart of the world. It's not a mind and a heart of Christ. Please join me in praying for this person and others like them in churches all across America. We need to draw them in with the love of Christ. Because they need to be changed. They need to get that heart of Christ. That's the best thing we can do for them. That's the very, very best thing we can do.

Where are you at in this whole process? Have you found your ministry? Are you still searching for your ministry? Maybe you haven't even accepted Christ as your savior yet? Wherever you are in this, at whatever point, my prayer today is take that next step. If you're a brand new Christian, I'm not expecting you to go to the mission field tomorrow. But I want you to take a step. Whatever it is that God has in your heart and your mind right now - it's different for everybody reading this book. But as you were reading, God put something in your heart. God put something in your head. Whatever that thing is, take that step. Take that step today. If it's something that I can help facilitate let me know. And I'll help you take that step. I will do whatever I can do to help you grow spiritually, whatever I can do. But you have to make the effort; you have to take the step. I can hold your hand along the way, but ultimately, it's the blind leading the blind because I'm still growing too. I can teach you what I know. I can show you and share with you what God has done in my life, but ultimately this is between you and Christ. Whatever he's telling you to do, do it. Whatever he's planted in your heart and planted in your mind, take that step. You know what it is, we don't have to play games - it's already in your heart. It was in your heart before you picked up this book, and as you were reading it got louder. And when I touched on it, it screamed. You know what it is; let's take that step today.

Let's Go Deeper

1. Who is your "Jerusalem" and what is your plan to reach them with the love of Christ?

2. Who is your "Judea" and what is your plan to reach them with the love of Christ?

3. Who is your "Samaria" and what is your plan to reach them with the love of Christ?

4. Who is your "Uttermost" and what is your plan to reach them with the love of Christ?

5. What ministries does your church have that you can be part of to tell the world about Jesus?

6. Write Acts 1:8 in the space below and make plans to memorize it this week.

For Pastors

Teaching about Others is a great time to invite a missionary family or two to your service. They can share the burden God has placed on their heart for the people of their "uttermost". It seems to help our congregation to see past their world. Also, if you are considering a mission trip, this is a great time to announce it. We had a great experience sending a team to work with Manna Worldwide in Guatemala last year. They start children's feeding centers alongside of new church plants. You can get more information about Manna at www.MannaWorldwide.com.

Also, it's a good idea to contact any Missionaries that you are already supporting and inquire about short-term mission opportunities in their field. Not only can you have a great experience for your people but they will get to see firsthand how their donations are being used.

CHAPTER 3 – FOCUS ON THE CROSS

The C in FOCUS is for the Cross. Our focus upon the cross is vital because the cross changed everything. Everything in our history and our future changed because of what took place on the Cross of Calvary. I think that too often Christians have a sterilized view of what took place on the cross. We get a sterilized image of the cross because when we hang a cross on the wall, we put up a cross that's been painted and stained and shined and waxed. And they look nice and pretty, but in actuality the cross was an instrument of torture. It was a device of death. I think we forget the agony that Jesus Christ felt as He approached his time upon the cross, where He was in the garden praying and agonizing over what was about to take place. And how He prayed, earnestly, that if there was any other way, if there was any way that He could avoid the cross...but He knew there wasn't...He knew the price that had to be made for all of mankind. I want to focus on how important the cross was/is for you. We forget about the mock trials. We forget about those that were paid to bring false testimony before him. We forget what He must've been going through when He stood before Pilate and when Pilate gave the people the option of freeing him or freeing the murderer Barabbas. Can you imagine what went on in His heart? God made flesh. He came to this earth to seek and to save that which was lost. While He was here, He healed thousands. He fed thousands. He helped and encouraged and changed and gave hope to a people that were without hope, and He stands before those people. And they cry out, "Crucify him!" After He had given them so much. After He had given everything. His Heart must have been broken. I don't know if I could've gone on beyond that. How did He not break down and weep?

Then we see the scourging and the beatings. We see the scourging where they take Jesus, a man who has no fault, who has no sin, who is being punished for something He never did, never even considered, and He's taken and placed over a log and his hands are secured, and they take the scourging whip and they whip him with the scourging whip. I don't know if you've ever seen a scourging whip or a picture of a scourging whip. When we get it in our mind, we think of a whip — we think of a bullwhip. Well, think of a bullwhip that's shorter but instead of 1 tip on it, it'll have 7 or 9 tips on it. And then instead of just a piece of leather on the end of that, a metal hook. Not like a fishing hook. More like a piece of sharpened angle iron that's on the end of each one of those tips. And when they would whip somebody with it, they would lay it across their backs. And those hooks would reach around and grab into the person's side. The hooks would dig into skin, and they would drag the scourging whip across the back. It was designed to be deep enough to cut through the skin and cut into the muscle, but not deep enough to where it would reach any of the major arteries to where it would actually kill a person. Why? Because they weren't trying to kill with the scourging whip. They were trying to torture. And the longer the person stayed alive, the better it was. And they whipped Him and whipped Him and whipped Him. The Bible doesn't tell us how many times. There's a thought out there that He was whipped 40 minus 1 because that was considered in Jewish tradition to be the limit that a human could withstand. But these weren't the Jews that were scourging him. These were the Romans. The Romans had no such tradition. We don't know if it was 39. We don't know if it was 40. We don't know if it was 100. All we know is He was beaten over and over.

And then they mocked Him. They took and put a robe on him and gave him a fake scepter. And they put a crown upon his head and pushed it down onto his skin, a crown of thorns. They came by one at a time, they mocked him, spit in His face, slapped Him, and punched him in his face. Then they made a cross and made him carry it. The cross didn't look like the one hanging on the wall of your church. The cross was a torture device. They would usually just take trees and split the logs so it was just unfinished wood. They would lash it together and make a cross out of it, and they made Him carry this cross the mile or so until He gets to Mount Calvary. Usually they would have to take the person and drag them to the cross. But Jesus went willingly. When the cross was laid down, He laid himself down upon that cross. Think about the pain of his recently scourged back, laying on that unfinished, jagged piece of wood. He laid down. They pulled him tight and nailed him to the cross. He never cried out. He never begged for them to stop. He went to the cross and gave up his life there. As He hung upon that cross, He prayed for the people that had beaten and abused Him. As He hung upon the cross, his Father couldn't bear to see anymore and as the sins of the World were being placed upon him, for the first time in his life, the Son was separated from the Father. As our sins are placed upon Him, the sky grew dark and the Son says, "My God, my God, why hast thou forsaken me?" All alone He died. God came to earth took on flesh, died for us. The Christ who ministered to us, died all alone.

The picture of the cross is hard for us to imagine. What we can imagine is shocking to us. It's startling to us. It's revolting to us, and yet we come together and we sing songs about it. That doesn't seem quite right, does it? To sing songs about this torturous act. This act that was more than just a physical torture. It was a public humiliation. To be crucified was humiliating for your family. It was humiliating for you. Today we try not to humiliate people when we punish. But then, part of the punishment was the humiliation. In most cultures, part of the punishment is the humiliation. Early in our country, we put people to the stocks, they were put in the public square locked in the stocks so that people could come by and throw things at them and abuse them and mock them. It was a form of degradation. That's what the cross was. The cross was humiliating, not the place for a King. Not the place for our Lord, not the place for God Himself, yet that's where He was: on the cross. The place where so many murderers and rapists and thieves and enemies of the state had been hung before. Now, our Jesus is hung there to die.

In spite of all that, a word is used in Hebrews chapter 12 to describe what Jesus felt on the cross that is just mind-boggling to me. Hebrews 12:2 says;

"Looking unto Jesus the author and finisher of our faith; who for joy that was set before him endured the cross, despising the shame, and is set down at the right hand of the throne of God."

Did you see that? *"for joy."* Now, I can think of a lot of words to describe the cross, if I was going to be crucified, if I was going to be publicly humiliated, I could think of a lot of words that describe the cross, but I don't think 'joy' would be the word I would use. Yet Jesus counted it "joy" to endure the cross. He incurred what looks to us to be the lowest point in history. But what looks to us to be the lowest point in his earthly life is actually the pinnacle of his life. His death was the pinnacle of his life, which is why He looked to it with joy. How? Why? John 17:1 says;

"Father, the hour is come; glorify thy Son that the Son also may glorify thee."

That's his prayer to the Father. Jesus is saying, "Father, I'm going to the cross with joy because it's going to glorify you." What's glorifying mean? It means to make known. By being crucified, He was making known, He was declaring His Father. Jesus went to the cross to make His Father known. He went to the cross so His Father could have the glory. This is something we pray every Sunday morning when we come together before the services. And when we pray, we don't pray, "Let the Pastor have the glory." Or, "Let singers or whoever's up here on stage, let them have the glory." We pray, "Father make us transparent and let You have the glory. Let us make You known today." Because if we do anything else besides make the Father known today and that love that He shared through his Son, we're doing Worship wrong. That's why we should have joy when we come to Church to Worship. We shouldn't come in and have a somber, man-centered, boring worship. Hymns should not be sung as funeral dirges. I like to have the music to be a little upbeat in Church because we're coming in to worship with joy because we're coming in here to glorify God. In other words, we're coming in to make God known to everybody who walks through the doors. And hopefully, hopefully you're carrying that out of the church walls, you're taking it to your neighbors, you're taking it to your coworkers so that you can have that joy of the cross as well. Not where your joy is in the pain and the suffering of the cross but your joy is in the fact that, through the cross, the Father and the Son were made known. That's the glory of God. That's how we glorify God. Through this, they knew what God was like. They knew that God was perfect. They knew that God's judgment on sin was perfect. Our culture today—we seem to want to glorify sin. We seem to want to make sin known. We say, "Well, some sins are worse than other sins," but that's not how God sees it. God sees sin all the same. And what we need to understand, what this world needs to understand is: it doesn't matter how big or how little the sin is, God has dealt with it. He dealt with it on the cross. He dealt with all of the big sins on the cross. He dealt with all the little sins on the cross. Because, for Him, it's not big sin, little sin. It's just sin. Most of the time of the Bible when God or Jesus is talking about sin, there's no "s" on the end of that word.

It's not "sins." We usually say "sins" because we know the abundance of them in our lives. But God doesn't classify them as individual sins. He just looks down and says, "Sin. It's sin." It's this thing called "sin" that Jesus Christ died for on the cross. It's because of God's perfect plan, His only plan. He died and made the Father known. He made sure we knew what His God was like. He made sure that we knew that God was willing to sacrifice everything for you. Think about that for a minute. What more could the Father have sacrificed than his only begotten Son? And He sacrificed his only begotten Son for me and for you. We worship a God that doesn't hate us. The world thinks God hates us. The world pictures God as this judgmental being that is just waiting to strike us down. That's not the God that we worship. We worship a God that is willing to sacrifice anything, that has sacrificed anything for you and for them and the very people that nailed him to the cross. He was willing to sacrifice everything. Our God, our savior.

The Devil does a good job of misrepresenting the nature and the character of God since the beginning of time, and we fall for it every time. We serve a God that we fear out of respect. But we don't have to fear because He's fearful. He's not a scary guy. Our God is a loving God, a caring God, a God who's willing to do anything for us.

We like to look to Jesus as the great teacher. We like to look to Jesus as the great healer. We like to look to Jesus as, you know, the friend of the sinner. We like to look to Jesus at all these things. But the highest pinnacle of His life here on this earth was his death when He died for us on the cross. Without that moment, without that point in history, nothing else He did matters. Does it really matter that He fed 5,000 people that are all dead today? What difference does it make? They're all gone. They had a full belly one day. We look at that and say, "Oh, that was such a wonderful thing." And it was a wonderful thing. I'm not trying to take anything away from it. It was an amazing miracle that Jesus did, but that wasn't his highest point. How about when He made the blind see? That's an amazing thing, isn't it? Can you imagine being blind your entire life and then being able to see? Have you seen the videos out there of the kids who are born without hearing, and they're able to put in that implant in and they can hear their mother's voice for the first time? They're all so excited! They can't believe they can hear their mom's voice! That's a great thing—to help the deaf to hear, to help the blind to see. That's an amazing thing, but it really means nothing without the cross. What about Lazarus? He raised Lazarus from the dead. Wasn't that a great thing? Not for Lazarus. You don't hear much from Lazarus after that. Lazarus was probably thinking, "Hey, I was on my way to heaven, and now I'm back here with my sisters. They're kind of nags." But that's an amazing thing: to bring life back from the dead. But that wasn't the pinnacle.

We spend millions—billions of dollars—in this country, recognizing the birth of Jesus. And what a miracle that is: that God Himself left heaven to take on flesh, to be born as a child. How amazing is that? But that's not the pinnacle. We treat it like it's the pinnacle, but that's not the pinnacle. The pinnacle is the cross. The pinnacle is the death, the burial, and the resurrection. Because without that, nothing else matters. That was the grand gesture. That was the grand act. It was the cross. That's why He could go with joy. He rejected any other means. Remember, Satan gave him an option. After He had fasted for 40 days, after He spent time in the wilderness: when He was tired, when He was hungry, when He was weak, Satan says, "Here's my shot." And He comes to him and He says, "You're here for the world, right? I'll give it to you. All you've got to do is bow down. Bowing down is an act of humility. Less humbling than the cross. It'd be easier to bow down than to go to the cross." But that wasn't the way. Jesus wasn't here to get salvation for us through Satan. He was here to bring us salvation through His own blood, the only way it would've really worked. On the cross, we see his final words. He says, *"It is finished."* His first recorded words in the Bible are recorded in Luke 2:49, *"How is it that ye sought me? Wist ye not that I must be about my Father's Business?"* His first recorded words were, *"I must be about my Father's business."* And we see for the next three and a half years, that's exactly what He did. He went about his Father's business. And when He got to the cross, and He died on the cross, his final words were, "It is finished. I've done it. I've achieved the pinnacle. I've carried out my Father's business. I've carried out my Father's plan. It's done." We look at those words sometimes *"it is finished"* like the gasp of a dying person. That last gasp and the sadness of the words, but those aren't sad words. Those are the most amazing words of all of creation: when Jesus Christ said, "It is finished." Those weren't words of defeat. Those were words of victory. He wasn't saying, "My life is finished." He wasn't saying, "I am finished." He's saying, "The victory is done. We have won! Everything that takes place after this, we are fighting a war that is already

won. We are fighting a defeated foe. Satan is defeated."
Sin is defeated because Jesus Christ finished it on the
cross.

Do you see why it's important to focus on the cross?
Do you see why it's important not to take our eyes off
the cross? Because that's where everything is hinged.
That's where everything changed. That's where history
was changed. That's where Jesus shouted for joy, "It is
finished." Why else would He go to the cross? Why else
could He go to the cross with joy? Because He knew that
the acts that took place on that cross, the sacrifice that
was made on that cross would set sinners free.
Remember why He came? To seek and to save that
which was lost. That was his mission statement here on
earth. He didn't come to heal. He didn't come to feed.
Those were just ways He accomplished his goal of
seeking and saving that which was lost. And that's what
He accomplished on the cross. We were slaves. Every
person in this world was a slave to sin, and He set us
free. We were guilty, and He cleansed us. We were
helpless, and He came to rescue us. His death
transformed us. His death took us out of our hopeless
condition and our impending death and gave us eternal
life.

We look at Jesus being transformed through the
resurrection, we see the transformation of history, but in
reality, what changed on the cross was our lives. My life
was changed because of that cross. Your life, if you've
accepted Jesus Christ as your savior, has changed
because of the cross. We can't lose sight of the fact that
what happened on that cross changed us. It gave us
value. It exposed our worth, the worth that the Father

had in us. Don't ever think that you're worthless. I talk to people and I see things posted on Facebook about people who feel so worthless. They talk about giving up. They think about just throwing in the towel, just being done with everything. God doesn't die for the worthless. What would be the point of dying for worthless? He didn't die for worthless. He died for you. You were created on purpose for a purpose. God loves you. Don't ever let Satan whisper in your ear that you're not worth something because you are worth everything that God had. You are not worth just a little bit. You're worth Jesus Christ dying for you on the cross. That should humble you. That should be humbling because when we look at ourselves we see the error. But, He knows you better than you do. The only one that knows you better than you is the one that died on the cross for you. We start to believe the lie in our heads that we're worthless, that we're not worthy because we know how bad we are. We know what we've done that nobody else knows. We know those things that we've done in our past that shame us, and we don't even want to talk about it. We know those things, and He knew those things. And He still looked at you and said, "You're still worth dying for." Amen. Isn't that amazing? That's the cross. That's what happened on the cross. He gave us a new life. He gave us a new eternal life. He gave us a new spiritual life. He gave us a new divine life. He gave us a way to be set free from sin. Throughout the history of the earth, mankind had been enslaved to sin. In the Old Testament the best that they could do was to have their sins covered at the temple each year, but it didn't free them from sin. They still wore the shackles of sin. The blood of animals didn't free them from their sin, it just covered up their sin for a year. But because of what took place on the cross, now humankind could be free from sin. We can be forgiven. You can be forgiven. It doesn't matter what you've done. It doesn't matter what you thought of doing. You can be forgiven. I sat down with a man one time, and I was talking to him about Jesus Christ. He started weeping, crying. He says, "I want to be saved so bad, but I can't. You don't understand what I've done. You don't understand what my past is." I said, "I don't care what your past is. I know what Jesus' past is, and He died for you." He says, "No, no. I've killed people." He says, "In Desert Storm, I killed people." He said, "I was a sniper in Desert Storm. I killed people." He felt so guilty about killing the people that He went to his chaplain and the chaplain told him, "There's nothing you can do. You can't be forgiven because you can't be forgiven in murder. You're going to hell." And he lived with that burden and that belief that he was not worthy because he had taken a life in battle. I don't care if you've taken a life in battle. I don't care if you've taken a life in the heat of passion. You're worthy, and you can be forgiven. That soldiers name was Tony and I am happy to say that Tony accepted Jesus Christ as his savior. Because Jesus Christ felt Tony was worth dying for.

You may be thinking "Well, Pastor, you don't know my sin." True, and I don't want to know your sin. You confess your sin to God, not man. You don't have to confess your sin to me. If you start confessing your sins to me, I'm a human, I may start looking at you funny. I won't tell anybody, but I'll be like "nu uh. I'm not getting in the car with that guy." I don't want to know your sin. Jesus already knows your sin, and He says you're worthy to be forgiven.

You are worthy to be forgiven and accept Jesus Christ as your savior. I'm guessing that since you are reading this you have some understanding of Jesus as your Saviour. You probably have some understanding of your sin. You have some understanding of your need of forgiveness. The tragedy is a lot of people stop with the understanding. They have the head knowledge that Jesus was God made man and that He died for their sins and arose out of the grave on the third day but they never believe it in their hearts. We're not called to be saved in our head. We're called to be saved by faith. Faith doesn't come from our head. Faith comes from the heart. Don't ever confuse head knowledge with heart faith. It's only about 18 inches between the head and the heart, but it's the distance of all of eternity. Some of us sit a mere 18 inches away from eternity. Never confuse it. Just because you've got the knowledge in your head does not mean that you're saved. But praise God. What it does mean is that you're 18 inches away. You're very, very close. It takes getting it out of your head and getting into your heart. There's nothing wrong with understanding the Gospel in your head. As a matter of fact, I encourage you to. That's one of the reason why I encourage people to constantly study their Bibles and why I am constantly taking classes and looking for wise men of God to learn from.

Many people don't know that early on I went to school to be an auto mechanic and I worked for several years as an auto mechanic at a couple of different dealerships in Lakeland, FL. Turns out that what I enjoyed and really loved as a hobby, I began to hate as a career. I don't even work on my own cars now unless I have to. If it doesn't break, it'll keep making noise until it does. I don't want to do anything with it. I even take it to somebody else to change the oil. I don't even want to deal with that. The point is, I have a lot of head knowledge about cars. I can tell you how a car works. I can tell you what each system in the car does. I can tell you what a car is supposed to do. I can tell you the difference between different types of engines. I can tell you what a straight 6 is, I can tell you want a slant 6 is. I can tell you what a rotary engine is and how they work. I can tell you all that. I understand cars inside and out. I'm not touching one, but I understand it. I can tell you the difference between a 4 stroke and 2 stroke engine. I can tell you how your fuel injectors work and why an alignment is important. I know a lot about cars, but no amount of knowledge will ever make me a car. I know more about the cars than the cars know about themselves. But I'm still not a car. It's not knowledge that makes you a car just like it's not knowledge that makes you a Christian. It's your faith in what Jesus Christ did on that cross, his death, his burial, and his resurrection. We're saved by His grace, not by our knowledge. You may have a whole head full of knowledge about the Bible. Praise God for that. Praise God that He gives us a head that'll hold a lot of knowledge. But none of that knowledge is going to save you unless that knowledge is put into faith. You have to have faith and trust in what Jesus Christ did on the cross to be saved.

It takes our faith and trust. When we call upon Him, when we go to Him and say, "God, I'm a sinner. And according to Your word and according to my heart, I should die to be eternally separated from you. I should die for my sins. That's what I deserve but I'm nothing but a sinner. But I believe. But I believe that Jesus Christ died for my sins." Not "I understand" but "I believe He died for my sins." And because of that, I can have eternal life. Have you done that? Have you accepted Jesus Christ? Have you accepted that free gift?

You should be able to think back to that time when you weren't saved. I talk to people a lot about salvation and there is a lot of confusion out there about salvation. I'll talk to somebody and they'll say, "Oh, I'm saved." But when I try to get clarification by asking when or where they accepted Christ or how old they were when they got saved I get some very concerning answers, some will say "Oh, I've always been saved." If you believe that you have always been saved then you're not saved. You should be able to look back and find that time when you were not saved and say, "This is when I got saved." Now, maybe you don't remember the day. Now, I'll tell you, when I got saved, I was a small child and I didn't write the date down. It was never documented. The church that I was saved in has been closed. It was merged with another church. Another church went into the building, and all the records are gone. So there's no records of my salvation where anybody wrote it down. I don't even know for sure if anybody at the church wrote it down, but I remember the day. I can't tell you for sure what day it was but God knows what day it was. It's written in His book, and it's written on my heart. I remember the place. I remember the time. I remember the person who led me to the Lord. I took my family back there a few years back. It was a Saturday and they were having a cookout. Isn't that a great time to stop by a church? On a Saturday when they're outside having a cookout. I introduced myself to the Pastor, explained why I was there and he opened the building to us. When we went inside of the church I found the Sunday School classroom where I accepted Christ as my Saviour. The room looked a little different, of course, they had painted and changed things a little, but I remember that room. There's nothing special about that room. It's not holy ground any more so than any other place on this Earth, but it's special in my heart because that's where I was when I met Jesus Christ. Do you have that place in your heart? Can we go back there? If we all got in a bus, could we go there? You should have that place. Because if you don't have that place, you need to ask yourself, "Am I really saved? Have I truly accepted or have I just assumed that I accepted Jesus Christ as my Saviour? I assume because I've been going to church. I've been around church people my whole life. I've assumed that I'm saved." Assuming that you're saved... Satan wins. Because that assumption keeps you from trusting that Jesus Christ is your savior. The Bible doesn't say that we can assume we have salvation. The Bible doesn't say that we can hope we have salvation. The Bible says that we can know that we have salvation. To know something is to not doubt something. To know something is to have it cemented in your mind. People can try to talk you out of something that you know, but you know it to be true. Because it's true. And that's why your personal testimony is the most powerful witnessing tool you have. Because the atheist can twist the word of God. Satan has been twisting the word of God since the Book of Genesis, and they've gotten good at twisting it. And they'll do their best to confuse Christians about the word of God. But you know what's the one thing they can't confuse? It's what you know. I know that Jesus Christ died for me. I don't care what anybody says. I don't care what any theologian says. I don't care what any atheist says. I don't care what any of you say. I know that Jesus Christ died for me, and I accepted Him as my Saviour. And that's it. That's it. There's nobody that can change my mind on that because I know. I was there.

I was in the room when my son was born. Nobody can convince me that he wasn't born. I've tried to convince myself a couple times that he was hatched, but I was there. I saw him when he was born. I know it to be a fact. There's nothing anybody can do to convince me differently. They can't take that away from me. They can't change my mind on that because I know. Do you know? Do you know if you've been forgiven? Have you repented of your sin and accepted Jesus Christ as your Saviour? Maybe in your heart you're saying, "I'm not sure." Don't lose your focus on the cross. Today is the day of your salvation. Today, not tomorrow. There may not be a tomorrow, but there is today. And today can be the day of your salvation.

Let's Go Deeper

1. What do you see when you visualize the cross of Calvary?

2. How was God's love made real on the cross?

3. When you think about God the Father, who do you see; a hateful, vindictive God or the loving, caring God described in the Bible?

4. Have you accepted the gift that was paid for you on the Cross?

5. In the space below, describe the place and time of your Salvation.

6. Write Hebrews 12:2 in the space below and make plans to memorize it this week.

For Pastors

The Cross. This was actually the sermon the Holy Spirit gave me first and all of the others revolve around focusing on the cross of Calvary. Consider building a large cross for your auditorium. If possible, place it in the middle and arrange the seats in a circular pattern extending out from the cross. Preach from a place behind or out of sight from the congregation so that they can be focused on the cross and the price that was paid on that torturous cross. If this is impractical, you will also get good results and make a lasting memory by having the cross at the front and directing attention to it as you share the story of the cross. This is likely to be a very emotional service, so have plenty of tissue on hand. As a further reminder, hand out small pocket crosses as your congregation leaves. This service lends itself to people accepting Christ as their Saviour, so make sure your Soul Winners are prepared and standing by!

CHAPTER 4 – FOCUS ON UNDERSTANDING

The U in FOCUS is for understanding. 2 Timothy 3:16 & 17, it says *"All scripture is given by inspiration of God, and is profitable for doctrine, for reproof, for correction, for instruction in righteousness: That the man of God may be perfect, thoroughly furnished unto all good works."* Back in World War II while our men and women were fighting, there was a group of ladies that started to broadcast over the radio. They played American music, rock and roll and pop music from that time, and it was broadcast to our troops. These women, collectively, were known as Tokyo Rose. Some of you may know the story and you may know how that there was one woman, an American, who was singled out in that group and was actually prosecuted in this country for treason. But it was actually a group of women whose purpose was to distort the message that was being sent to our troops. They were to come in and very, very subtly they were to change things just a little bit, and put a little bit of doubt in the minds and the hearts of our troops, because they knew that if they could plant those seeds of doubt, that the doubt would

67

grow. Praise God, most of our men that were serving overseas knew what was taking place and they just shrugged it off. But those seeds of doubt were planted in some. And some were made less effective and some were made completely ineffective because those seeds of doubt that were planted began to grow.

We look back at that and see how bad that was but understand, that's been Satan's primary job since the very, very beginning; to change God's Word and plant those seeds of doubt. Notice when he came to Eve in the garden, what did he do? He used God's word against her. But he changed it just a little bit. He changed it a little bit and where Eve's failing was, and where some of those men in World War II failed, was that they were getting their understanding from the wrong source. If we want to understand God, we need to get our understanding of God from God. Too many Christians today get their understanding of the Bible from the world. They allow the world to tell them what to think about marriage. They let the world tell them what to think about the church. They let the world tell them what to think about Jesus Christ. The world has no authority in those areas. The world has no authority in any area that God has claimed as His. When somebody in the world starts to try and instruct you on what the church should be or what Jesus Christ was really like, you need to turn that off and go to a better source for your understanding. Go to a better source *of* understanding. Go to the word of God. Go to the scriptures that God gave us for that purpose. We've all heard the lies. We've all heard the lines. I was told one time I need to be more like Jesus. I agree. You're not going to get an argument out of me there. That's my goal: to be more like Jesus. But I asked them to explain. What are you talking about? Jesus always loved people. Jesus never judged people. Jesus never spoke badly of people. And I had to stop them and I had to say, "Who are you talking about?" Because you don't know who the Jesus of the Bible is. I can start acting more like Jesus, you hypocrite, you viper. Let me go get my whip and beat you with it and chase you around the room. I can act more like Jesus.

The internet's a great thing, but people will try and pull you into spiritual conversations that suit their purposes. I had a person that tried to do that to me once; he was actually a friend of a friend and it was something on a post and he was trying to "enlighten" me to his spiritual truth. I stopped him and asked, "Where did you go to church on Sunday?" He replied, "I don't go to church." I said, "Okay, well don't take offense to this but I don't get my theology from people that are standing in disobedience to God." We need to be very careful where we get our understanding from because the world will give us something that feels right. The world will give us something that sounds right, but if it contradicts the Word of God, it's 100% wrong, every single time.

Be careful where you get your understanding from. God gave us a book. Actually, God gave us 66 books. The word 'bible' indicates that it's actually many tomes of work. It's many books. There are 66 different books in the word of God. God used about 39 human authors to record His word. But make no mistake about it, the author of every single one of those 66 books is God himself. The men that were used to write it, they were just simply pens in His hand. That's why if you start the book of Genesis and you read through the bible, you get the feeling that it was all written by the same person – because it was. And yet the men that God used were very, very different people. We had kings writing the bible. We had extremely poor people writing the bible. We had murderers writing the Bible. We had good old country pastors writing the Bible. Amos is one of my favorites. Amos is just an old country preacher. When you read it, you get that feeling from it. God used very, very different people. He used people who had problems with depression. He used people who were going through huge turmoil in their life. He used people who were sitting on top of the world. He used people who had persecuted Christians and he used people who would sacrifice everything for the name of God. And yet we see that common thread of God's love that runs through the entire Bible. There's about 2000 years from when the first pen was put to paper until the last pen was pulled from the paper. Most of the authors of the Bible had never read any of the other works that were presented in the Bible, and yet it reads as one work. There's never been a book that has been scrutinized more. There has never been a collection of books that people have ever been persecuted more for. More money has gone into, and more time and hours and sweat and tears have gone to disproving these 66 books than any other work that man has ever created, and it's found without error. When man imagines an error and in glee thinks he finds an error, it just takes a little bit of understanding, a little bit of prayer, and a little bit of research to find that God's Word is always perfect.

Modern science is still catching up to the science of

the Bible. When God said that the earth was round and hung up on nothing, modern science said that it wasn't round. It was flat and it was riding around on the back of a giant turtle. It took them a little while to get caught up. Now they realize the earth is round and it hangs upon nothing. Imagine that. It's without error. It is perfect. I use the King James Bible exclusively. There is a very simple reason for that – there is not an English version of the Bible that is more accurate and truer to the original scripture, the original writings, than the King James Bible. There just isn't. The only people that you'll get to debate that and argue with it are the ones that wrote the new versions. They'll argue with you. They'll say "This one's more perfect." Well who wrote it? "Well I did." I want the one written by God.

If every version is different than they cannot all be The Word of God. I had a Pastor tell me once, "If it's not the same then it's different. And if it's different, it's not the same." How simple is that? If it's different, if this one is the Word of God and this other one is different, then this isn't the word of God. It's different. So we stick with what's the most perfect. The pushback is always: "Well, the other versions are easier to read." That's true. Some of them are. Some of them aren't. I don't even understand what some of them are writing about because they have to change so much just to get a copyright so they can make money off of it. If they don't change enough, they have to go back in and make more changes to it.

If you're going to translate the word of God, your sole purpose needs to be to spread the word of God, not to make money off of it. I don't mind people selling

71

Bibles. There are a lot of expenses that go into printing Bibles. I don't have a problem with a publisher printing and selling Bibles. But if that's your purpose, just to make money, you're starting out tainted. You're starting out wrong.

We need to get our understanding from the Word of God, and easy to read is not a qualification. I remember when I first started learning how to read, remember the Dick and Jane books? See Dick run, see Jane run. They chase the ball. The ball is blue. Those books are easy to read but they're not the Word of God. Easy to read doesn't equate to Word of God. It doesn't necessarily negate the Word of God. We'll talk a little bit more about the understanding of the Word of God and why it may be difficult for you to read the Word of God in just a moment because there may be a legitimate reason why it's difficult for you to read and why it's difficult for you to understand; a couple reasons, actually.

How do we understand the Bible? We know God gave it to us. We know it's the source of our understanding. Most of us have a Bible. We should all have one. Some of us have several. But just having it isn't what we're called to do with it. Having it isn't going to help us live our lives. We have to understand it. There are some simple things that we can do with this Word of God to make sure that we get the very, very most out of it. So that way when the world comes and tries to tell us something, we can say that's not right. That's not right, because I know what the Word of God says. And if it's different from the Word of God, it doesn't matter what it is. It's not right.

The first thing is, you've got to read it. You've got to read the Word of God. You need to read it. Jeremiah 15:16 *says "Thy words were found, and I did eat them; and thy word was unto me the joy and rejoicing of mine heart; for I am called by thy name, O Lord God of hosts."* Jeremiah, he had the right idea. He says "God, I found your Words. I'm eating them." He didn't mean he was tearing pages out and chewing them up. What he meant was as they came out of God's mouth, he was consuming them. He couldn't get enough of them. Think about after you've fasted for a while. If you've ever done a 3 or 4 day fast, you're hungry. And then there at the end, I'll tell you what happens to me, there at the end I'm not hungry anymore. I'm hungry that first day. That first day man, talk about a prayer life. I used to fast when I was driving around the country and it would never fail, you see every fast-food restaurant in the world when you're fasting and you've got to pray a lot because the steering wheel starts to turn and it starts to pull you into the drive thru. You've got to resist it. Get behind me, Burger King, and get back on track. Your prayer life will grow that first day. But after the first day, your hunger goes away, and you're able to focus upon God. It declutters the mind and it takes those things out of the mind to where you're able to focus upon God without having to worry about where your meals are coming from, without having to worry about where that money is going for this or for that. You get uncluttered. Where I run into problems is when I break the fast. When the fasting is done and it's time to reintroduce food back into your life there is a right way and a wrong way to do it. The right way is to start with liquids like broth and gradually work back up to solid foods. I don't have time to do all of that; I just start eating. And, unfortunately, what happens is that even though I'm not hungry, as soon as food gets in my mouth, I become ravenous. Now I'm real hungry and I want all can get. That's the picture I get of Jeremiah. That he had a little bite of God's Word and now he can't get enough. The buffet is not big enough. He's got to have more. As it's coming out of God's mouth, he's consuming it. That's how we should be with the Word of God. We need to stop looking at the Word and saying, "How much do I have to read today?" and instead start saying, "How much do I get to read today?"

Start planning out times to read your Bible. You need to have a plan in place to read your Bible, whether it's first thing in the morning, last thing at night, or on your lunch hour. I could give you pros and cons for different times of the day when you should read your Bible, but the short answer is to find a time every single day and make it your time. Have a plan. If you just say, "I'm going to read my bible more this month," you're not going to read it more. But if you say, "I'm going to take 15 minutes of my lunch every day and I'm going to read the Bible for 15 minutes," you know what you're going to do? You're going to read the Bible more this month because you've got a plan. Have a plan. People say, "What parts do I read?" Read all of it. Read the entire thing. If you're a new Christian, start with the book of John. Then go through the book of Romans. Those are good places to start. You don't have to start in Genesis, but you can. You need to have a plan to read it. There are plans all over the internet. You can either read it by starting at the beginning and working to the end, or you can get a chronological reading plan. I like the chronological plan myself because it takes the Bible in the order that the incidents occurred. You jump around a little bit but it takes you in order. It helps me to see how things fit together in the Word of God. If you do about 3 chapters a day, you can read your entire Bible through in a year. Just 3 chapters. That's really not that much. There's power in just reading the Word of God. You say, "I don't understand everything." It doesn't matter if you understand it. The Word of God, by itself, without any understanding, is powerful, immensely powerful. If you want to change the feel of your house, when you read, start reading it out loud.

Some of you know that two doors down from my house, a demonic cult moved in. This demonic cult sacrifices chickens and goats and other things to their gods. I can hear them down there when they get together for their annual celebrations. And when they first moved in I could feel it in my house, before I even knew what was going on. Our dog would sit in the doorway and stare down the hall that faced their property, like she could see something that I couldn't. The dog knew. The dog knew something was wrong. After I found out what was taking place it made more sense why my property and my house had this feeling of emptiness and eeriness. You know how I got rid of that eerie feeling? I started reading the Word of God out loud; I started praying out loud. I took my property back. I took our house back. There's great power in just reading the Word of God. Whether you read it out loud or read it silently, there is power just in that. That alone will transform your life just reading it. Read it. I encourage you to read it.

Some of the people say, "Well, I don't understand it." Well John 14:26 tells us this. He says, ***"But the*** *comforter, which is the Holy Ghost, whom the Father will send in my name, He shall teach you all things, and bring all things to your remembrance, whatsoever I have said unto you."* Two things I want you to understand about this verse. First, the Holy Spirit is the one that's going to teach you about the Bible. If you're not understanding anything in the Bible, you may not have the Holy Spirit. We get the Holy Spirit at the point that we accept Jesus Christ as our savior. So if you don't have the Holy Spirit, you're not saved. But if you've accepted Jesus Christ as your savior, you've got the Holy Spirit. Rely upon him to show you what you need to know out of the Word of God. Rely upon him. The second thing is it says that he brings it into remembrance. What does that mean? That he takes things and he brings them into our minds. If you've read the Bible for any length of time, you know what I'm talking about; when you're in a situation and suddenly a verse floats to the surface of your consciousness, and you're like wow, I didn't even know that verse was in there. And maybe it's just a piece of a verse, it's just a little bit of what God had to say about a situation, and it floats to the top. That's the Holy Spirit doing his job of helping you to remember what it was that you read.

Now think through this with me. If you've never read it, He can't bring it into remembrance. That's why it's important to read all of it. You say, "Well this doesn't really apply to me today." It might apply to you tomorrow. "I don't understand this." You might need to understand it tomorrow. The Holy Spirit may call it to your remembrance tomorrow and you'll be like, "That's what that means! Thank you, Jesus. Thank you for your Word." We've got to read it.

First you need to read His Word. Secondly you need to memorize some of it. Psalms 119:11 says, *"Thy word have I hid in mine heart, that I might not sin against thee."* This takes it to a little bit different level. This isn't just reading the Word. Now we're hiding the Word in our hearts. We use a different word for that usually. We don't say, "Are you hiding the Word in your heart?" What we'll normally say is, "Are you memorizing scripture?" Some of you, in your mind just said, "I can't remember my phone number, how am I going to memorize the Bible?" Praise God for cell phones. I don't even have to remember my phone number anymore. You don't have to remember your phone number but you can memorize the Word of God. You say, "Well it's hard for me to memorize." Your brain is like a muscle; the more you use it the stronger it becomes. And when you don't use it, it becomes weak. What I'm talking about is if you only tax your mind to do the same thing every single day, then your mind becomes stagnant. Your mind becomes stale. You have to challenge your mind. That's why as people get older their doctors will encourage them to do things like crossword puzzles because it forces their minds to think outside of the normal areas that they operate in and it helps them to maintain the longevity of their minds, so that hopefully their minds will last as long as their bodies do. That's the same way with memorizing scripture verse. If you haven't memorized scripture verse since you were a little kid, it's going to be hard at first. It's going to be really hard. But just because it's hard doesn't excuse you from doing it. Hide it in your heart. It may take you a month to learn one verse. Praise God, you learned a verse in a month! Start memorizing it. Again, just like reading, have a plan. Figure out where you are. If you memorize very,

very easily, then make it a more aggressive plan. If it's very, very tough for you, then give yourself some time. Memorizing verses isn't supposed to be beating yourself up. Take your time. Write it. Read it. Say it out loud and pick a verse. When you're reading the Word of God, verses are going to jump out at you. Pick one of those. You want a good one to start with? Start with John 3:16. That's the Bible in a nutshell right there. You say, "I've already got that." Well praise God! See? You can memorize something, right? Then move on to another verse. Find one that God wants you to memorize. Find a good verse for you.

I call certain verses in the Bible pocket verses because what I used to do when I memorized them. I would write them on a piece of paper and put the paper in my pocket so that every time I would put my hand in my pocket, I'd touch that piece of paper, and it would remind me of that verse. I would take the card out and read the verse over and put it back in my pocket. And it started to stick in my head. Now I call them my pocket verses. I'll be in certain situations and those are the verses God brings to my mind first, I praise God for my pocket verses. We need to memorize Scripture. Find those verses that the Spirit is illuminating and memorize them.

By the way, when you're reading, when you're working your way through the Bible, particularly as a new Christian, you're going to find a lot of parts in the Bible that you don't understand, and that's okay. There's nobody that understands everything about the Bible. So don't get hung up on the parts that you don't understand. Get hung up on the parts of the Bible that you do understand. Take those verses. Memorize those verses. Apply those verses. Focus on those verses. If you're reading your Bible every day and you're getting one verse every day out of those three chapters, only one verse is coming to you, that could sound frustrating, right? There's about 30 verses in a chapter, so you're reading almost 100 verses and you're finding only one that you understand. That can be a little discouraging, that can be a little taxing, and that can make you want to stop reading your Bible. But don't look at it that way. Don't look at the ones you don't understand. God gave you that one verse today, and that one verse is all you need today. Take that one verse that He gave you today and use that one. How dramatically will your life be changed if every day if you understand and apply one verse into your life? That's 365 small changes God has poured into you. You will be transformed.

After you've read your Bible through in a year and you go back and you're reading through the book of John the second time, you're going to see that one verse and think, "I know that verse. God used that verse this year. He gave me that verse and I used it 3 or 4 times this year." But here's what the great thing is – when you read those chapters again, instead of only getting 1 out of 100, now you're going to get at least one more. You may get 2 or 3 more. Eventually you'll start to say, "I got this chapter. I understand what He's talking about here. I see in His mind. I can see the picture He's painting here." And then the great thing is when you go back the next year and you read it again, you'll be like "I see something completely different now. It's bigger than I thought. I thought I had it and praise God it's even bigger than what I thought it was." I can't tell you how

79

many times I have read a verse in the Bible and said "I've never seen that before." You know why I never saw it? Because I didn't need it. It wasn't important for me at that time; now it is. And if I don't need it now, I'm about to need it. God is getting me ready. God is preparing me. He's giving me what I need, even before I need it.

We have to read God's Word. We have to memorize God's Word. And, we have to study God's Word.

2 Timothy 2:15 says: *"Study to show thyself approved unto God, a workman that needeth not to be ashamed, rightly dividing the word of truth."*

The third thing is we have to Study the Word of God. It's great to read it. There's power in reading it. There's power in memorizing it. But you've got to study the Bible. You've got to see how a certain Psalm interacts with a passage in Samuel or what is he talking about when he says the seed of the woman is going to bruise of Satan. You need to see how that connects with the crucifixion and start to put these things together by studying your Bible. Get a good study Bible or get some good commentaries. There are some good online resources. Matthew Henry wrote an amazing commentary on the Bible and there are many others. My only word of caution with commentaries is to understand that the commentaries weren't written by God. They were written by men. So a commentary is great, but understand that a commentary may have mistakes in it. I'll go a step further. A commentary will have mistakes in it because it was written by a man. It may be a good man. Dr. Willington out of Liberty

University is a great man of God, if you ever have the opportunity I encourage you to listen to him or talk to him. Elmer Towns, another great man of God, who helped found Liberty University. I've talked to Elmer Towns a few times and he'll bring up things and we'll start talking about things, and my head's spinning because he has lived it for so many years. But you know what, he's not perfect, he's a man. Be careful when it's a commentary, even if it's a commentary by a well-respected, very knowledgeable person. Understand they're men. And where I don't think that either one of those men that I mentioned would ever purposely mislead, they're men and they make mistakes. Keep that in mind. I'm not saying dismiss all the commentaries because there are some very, very good commentaries out there. What I like about commentaries is that they help me to see the scripture from somebody else's point of view. I get to see what God shared with somebody else, and that's a great thing. That's powerful.

A key phrase in 2 Timothy 2:15 is *"rightly dividing."* We need to rightly divide the Word of God. This is important. When you're studying the Word of God, you need to ask yourself some questions about the Word of God.

When you're looking at a particular passage, you need to ask yourself:

Who is speaking here? Who is it that's talking? Because even though all the scripture is given for us, and there is a purpose in it, not all of it is talking directly to us. Sometimes we're seeing people talk to other people and we're getting both sides of the conversation and one side is the right side and the other side is the wrong side; we need to understand who it is that's talking.

Who is it that is being talked to? Don't make a command about you that was written specifically to a single person or a certain people group.

What is taking place during that time? What exactly is happening at that time? What is it that's going on? Because there are commands all through the Bible where the illustrations are great, where the meaning is great, but it's not a command for us today. Here's a good example for you. In Egypt, when the final plague is coming through, there's a command in the Bible to take blood and hyssop and put it on our door posts. Did any of you do that this week? It's a command in the Bible. Why didn't you do it? Because God's not talking to us, is He? That's not for us, is it? It's a command in the Bible, a command from God in the Bible, but it's not for us. But there's a picture there that's valuable for us. We see the picture that we are covered by the blood of Jesus Christ just as the first born in those houses were covered by the blood of that lamb; we are covered by the blood of the perfect lamb. It is valuable for us. There is a lesson. There is an understanding to be had but the direct command is not for us. We need to be careful when we're rightly dividing.

We need to read in context. Taking a command out of context leads to dangerous theology. Look at Daniel 3:11, *"And whoso falleth not down and worshippeth, that he should be cast into the midst of a burning fiery furnace."* I'm going to take this verse literally out of context and I'm going to say if you do not fall down and worship God today, we're going to build a furnace and you're going in it. Isn't that what it said? Isn't that what it says in Daniel 3:11? *"And whoso falleth not down and worshippeth, that he should be cast into the midst of a burning fiery furnace."* I made a lot of errors with that verse though, didn't I? What's the first error? I pulled it out of context for one thing. Also, that was Nebuchadnezzar speaking, not God. Is Nebuchadnezzar a good source of scriptural understanding? He was an evil king, wasn't he? Nebuchadnezzar is probably not where we want to get our commandments from, to start with.

You've got to rightly divide the Word when you study the Word. Here's a tip for you. In your studies if you find two parts in the Bible that seem to contradic each other, study some more or get some help, because the Bible never contradicts itself, because it's all written by the same author.

We have to read God's Word. We have to memorize God's Word. We have to study God's Word. And, we have to hear the Word of God.

Luke 11:28 says: *"But He said, yea rather, blessed are they that hear the word of God, and keep it."* I want to focus on that first part first. We'll get to the rest of that in a moment. First it says, *"blessed are they that hear the word of God."* We need to hear the Word of God. Not just read it, not just study it, we need to hear it. That's my job on Sunday morning from the pulpit. Sunday Morning Worship should be part of your hearing the Word of God but, it shouldn't be all of it. If you're only hearing the Word once a week you are going

83

to be starved by the end of the week. But Sunday Worship is a vital part; it is an opportunity for you to hear the Word of God. One of the great things about living in the age we live in today is that we have an unprecedented opportunity to hear the Word of God. We have the greatest opportunity ever in the history of the world to hear the Word of God, because we have access 24 hours a day, 7 days a week, to preaching on the Word of God. You must be discerning about what you listen to because most of what's out there, most of what's on TV, radio or internet is not fit to watch or hear. But look for men that stand up and preach the pure Word of God and rightly divide it and start putting those into your ears. Download them and listen to them in your car, or find a radio station that has good Bible preaching on it. Listen to that in your car. There are some good ones. I have some that I like to listen to. I don't know if we're supposed to play favorites with pastors or not, but I have favorite pastors out there I like to listen to. I enjoy listening to Tony Evans. He pastors a church in Dallas. He can pull apart the Bible and explain it in the simplest terms and put it all back together again. He does an amazing job, with a lot of passion in his preaching. I love that. There's Paul Chapel. Pastor Chapel out of Lancaster Baptist Church in Lancaster, California. I don't think he's on the radio but he's on the internet and you can download and watch his services on the internet; a powerful man of God. Of course there's this other guy who Pastors a growing country church in Florida that you will probably enjoy at LifeAtTheCrossroads.com. Find these guys. They're out there. Don't just use Sunday Morning as the only time you hear the Word. Seek out other resources. Maybe your church records teachings online.

We have to read God's Word. We have to memorize God's Word. We have to study God's Word. We have to hear the Word of God. And we have to keep the Word of God.

The last part of that verse in Luke 11:28 says, **"and keep it."** We have to keep the Word of God. This is probably the most important piece but you got to have those other pieces in place to get to this piece. What does it mean to keep the Word of God? It means to live by the Word of God, to apply the Word of God. It means to take those things that God has illuminated to you and instill them in your life. To take that one verse that He gave you today, that one nugget, that one thing that He gave you and build that into your life. As I mentioned before I'm trying to become more like Christ. I'm not Christ. I'm not even worthy of being on the same planet or the same universe with Christ. That's how far away from Him I am. But my goal is to be like Christ. That's what the word "Christian" means, it means that we're on a journey to become more Christ-like. How do we do that? We take those things that He gives us and we take those small steps to get closer and closer to Christ every single day. That's keeping it. That's applying it. That's living the Word of God. If you're coming to church like an angel on Sunday morning and then living like the devil the rest of the week, you're missing it. You're missing the power of living a life in Christ. You're missing the power and the comfort of knowing that God's out there for you, that you're not out there bobbing around, waiting for everything in the world to hit you and knock you around, that you've got somebody that will never leave you, that will never forsake you, that you've got that person that will always be there. And He's not a person like me that's going to make mistakes. He's perfect in everything that He does. He can see tomorrow so He can prepare you for what's coming. He can help you take every step. That's my goal as a Pastor, to help you take a step. That, more than anything else, is what I try to help you do every single week; take a small step. If you want to take a big leap, praise God for that. But if I can get everybody to take a small step…what are your small steps this week? How are you going to increase your understanding of His Word?

Let's Go Deeper

1. How do you plan to read through the Bible this year?

2. Other than the verses you are memorizing through this book, what is your plan to continue to memorize God's Word on a regular basis?

3. What is your plan to Study God's Word? What Bible Commentary will you use?

4. If you don't already attend a Bible teaching church, make a plan to find one. Pray to God and visit several in your area. Email me at; PastorJay@LifeAtTheCrossroads.com and I will help you find one in your area.

5. How does the world see God's Word lived out in your life?

Jay McCaig

6. Write II Timothy 3:16 in the space below and
   make plans to memorize it this week.

For Pastors

Have on hand Bible reading plans that your congregation can use. I like to give them options such as the entire Bible in a year or the New Testament in a year, and I also like a chronological reading plan, but choose whatever you think your people will embrace. Set up a system of rewards to help keep them motivated along the way and provide a certificate when they make it through the year. This is also a great time to kick off a new Small Group or even a Bible Institute in your Church. Several colleges offer distance learning in print and online for degree and certificate programs. Encourage your leaders to avail themselves of these classes, perhaps even splitting the cost as an investment in their ministry at the church. Lead by example; how long has it been since you left seminary? Maybe it's time to stretch yourself once again and take a class or two on a subject you need a refresher on. Growing churches are led by growing Pastors. I recommend Louisiana Baptist University, www.LBU.edu, because of their adherence to biblical doctrine and the low cost. There are many other good schools out there; find one that meets your particular needs.

CHAPTER 5 – FOCUS ON SALVATION

The S in FOCUS is for Salvation. Jesus said that He came to the world to ***"seek and to save"*** the lost, and that is what He did. Through His death we have the power to be saved. But there is a condition that must be met. I John 1:9 says, ***"If we confess our sins, he is faithful and just to forgive us our sins, and to cleanse us from all unrighteousness."*** You see there is a condition that must be met on our part. We have to confess our sins. Romans 10:10 says: ***"With the mouth confession is made unto salvation."*** God is not under any obligation; if we don't confess our sins, there is no obligation to save us. There is the thought in the world today that since God is a good and loving God that he will never send anybody to hell. That is not what I John 1:9 says. That verse says that we have to confess our sins if we want salvation. If we chose not to confess our sins, if we chose not to accept that free gift of salvation, God doesn't send us to hell; we chose to send ourselves to hell. It has got to be so frustrating for him. He must stand there bewildered saying, "I did everything for you. I sent my only begotten son for you.

He sacrificed his life for you. He paid the price for you. I created this entire heaven for you and you chose to reject it."

The Bible only knows of two places; it knows of heaven and it knows of hell, that's it. When we stand before God and we have rejected heaven, the only thing left is hell. There is nothing in between, there is no limbo, there is no purgatory, there is no Nirvana; these are all places created in the minds of man. They do not exist. When we die, we don't have the option of going into a waiting area. We either go to heaven or we go to hell, that's it. When we deny God's way and try to achieve salvation our own way: *"I want to get to heaven by being a good person"*, or *"I am going to get to heaven by going to church"*, or *"I am going to get to heaven by donating money"*; when we chose our way instead of His way, our way leads into hell, every single time. It is up to us. We have to choose to confess our sins if we want to be saved.

If we confess, John 1:12 tells us that we have the **"power to become the sons of God."** The mindset that God wouldn't send anybody to hell, that God wouldn't condemn anybody to hell, that is that same mindset that says we are all God's children; but the Bible doesn't say that we are all God's children. The bible says something very contrary to that. The bible talks about our father being Satan (John 8:44). Now don't get me wrong, every single one of you was created by God, on purpose, for a purpose. You were lovingly created by God and God loves you more deeply than you will ever understand, every single one of you, but that does not make you a child of God. John 1:12 says that he gave us the power to become the sons of God.

If we have the power to become something that means that we are not already that thing. We can't become something that we already are. You see, through the power, through the price that was paid on the cross, we have the power to become the sons of God. We have the power. He placed it into our hands, to make the decision of whether or not we are adopted into his family. We have the power but we must confess our sins.

Our confession must be genuine; it can't be a half-hearted confession. Confession is not just making a list of our sins. It isn't saying, I'm a liar, I'm a cheater, I'm a thief, I'm a robber; it is not just making a list of our sins, because that is easy to do. We can all make a list. If I gave you a piece of paper and a pen and guaranteed you that nobody else would ever see it, you could probably make a pretty good list. Then as you went back into your head and started thinking about when you were younger and things you did when you were a teenager and the things you did maybe even before that, and you started remembering all the way back to yesterday and the sins you committed then, you could probably make a pretty good list and you could probably make it pretty quick. If you did share this list, you would probably be surprised at how shockingly similar your sins are to other people around you. Do you know why? Because we are all sinners and although there is a great diversity of sin, they all boil down to rebellion against God.

It needs to be a complete confession. It is not a pick and choose confession. When we stand before God and confess our sins, it's got to be a complete confession. It's got to be a sincere confession. When someone claims Christ at their lowest point I sometime wonder if they are accepting Christ because they are truly repentant or because they got caught. My wife and I raised three teenagers. Sometimes it seems like we are still raising three teenagers; none of them are teenagers anymore, none of them live with us, but we are doing it by phone now, we are still trying to raise teenagers. Some of you can relate. When they were younger and we would catch them doing something wrong, they were always repentant, they were always sorry about it. We are blessed with grandchildren now, and our granddaughter, every time she gets caught doing something wrong, the first thing out of her mouth is, "I'm sorry grandpa, I'm sorry grandma." Very quick. She's quick to say she is sorry, but you know what? If we don't catch her, she is not coming to tell us she is sorry. She is sorry she got caught, not for what she did. When we go before God, we shouldn't go before God because we are sorry we got caught doing something wrong, we should be going before God because we are wrong. We have sinned against Him. Not against me, not against you; we have sinned against God. I have people, relatives, that know I am a Baptist Pastor. And sometimes when I am talking to them one of them will curse and the first thing that they do when they curse is, they apologize to me. I tell them you don't have to apologize to me when you sin, because you are not offending me, you are not sinning against me, you are sinning against God apologize to God. If you do something wrong, you don't have to come and apologize to me. If you stole something from me, you don't have to apologize to me, just give it back and apologize to God because you didn't sin against me, you sinned against God. We offended God and our confession is to be a complete confession to Him.

When we go before God and we confess our sins, our mindset has to be, I am not going to sin anymore. Now you know, if you have lived a Christian life; that we do sin. Hopefully it is not as much as before and hopefully you have a more difficult time sinning, but we still sin; regardless, our intention has to be that we are not going to sin anymore. That's got to be the heart that we bring to God. "God I am putting down this bottle," "God I am putting down this crack pipe," "God I am turning off the computer," "God I am going to do this or I am not going to do that." Whatever that thing is, our intention has to be, putting it away. If we continue to hold onto those things we are not really giving them to God.

When playing with a cat it is fun to take one of their toys and tie a string to it. Then slowly drag it along the floor and when the cat pounces, snatch it away. The cats love it and it plays to their natural instinct to hunt. That is how we act with our sins sometimes. We stick out our sins and say, here God, here is my sin, I want you to take my sin away from me God. But our sins have become so comfortable that as soon as God starts to take it, we snatch it back away and say, "no not this one, this is my pet sin. This one is the one that defines me; this is the one that is who I am. I am going to hold onto this one, God." Our sin has to be completely confessed. Notice what John says here. He doesn't say, if we confess our sin, he says, "if we confess our sins." Now prior to that, he was talking about sins and he addressed sin in a singular form, but here he uses it in a plural form because when we go before God, our confession has to be complete, we have to completely confess. We can't pretend that that one sin is not there and that that sin doesn't exist, "I am going to give you a nice list God, but don't touch that one. That one is mine, we are not even going to talk about that one. We are not going to discuss that one. You don't even have any business even thinking about that one God, that one is mine." When we give him 90% of our list, that's not confessing our sins; that is an incomplete confession. An incomplete confession does not obligate God to forgive you in any way, shape, or form. That is called incomplete or partial obedience.

Partial obedience is always complete disobedience. We like those gray areas that we pretend exist between obedience and disobedience. I am in the middle, but I am closer to obedience than I am to disobedience, I am almost there so I am better than all the other people who are just in complete disobedience. I at least read my bible and I go to church and I am almost there, I am close, I am a good person, I am almost there. If you are not in obedience, everything else is disobedience. There are no shades of gray with God; everything is black and white. Shades of gray is the world, that is the description of the world, that is the description of what is to be avoided. The Bible and God, they are black and they are white; there are no shades of gray. *"If we confess our sins, he is faithful and just to forgive us our sins"* I John 1:9. Listen to that again, *he is faithful and just to forgive us our sins.* Don't you love that? You see I said before that God is not under any obligation to forgive your sins if you will not confess. But, He is under obligation if you confess your sins. He has placed Himself under obligation, by the very nature of who he is, as being the perfect Holy God. By being the perfect Holy God he is under obligation, when we do what he has asked us to do, to do what he has promised to do because to do anything less would make him less than Holy; to do anything less would make him less than worthy. He is perfect. *"If we confess our sins, he is faithful and just to forgive us our sins."*

Conversion is a three-step process. The first step is, we have to confess. We confess and we turn from our sins. That confession and turning from our sins we call "repentance". Repentance is a word that a lot of people don't understand. Very simply, repentance is an action, repentance means to turn away from, and it is a movement. So when we repent, what we are doing is, we are turning away from our sins. In other words, I am moving away from my sin, both in my heart and physically, whatever it takes; I am moving away from my sin, we are repenting, but we are not just moving away and moving to nothing. That is what a New Year's resolution or turning over a new leaf does. That is incomplete repentance because it turns to nothing, and it creates a Spiritual vacuum. Nature abhors a vacuum, something always rushes in to fill them. If we do not choose what we turn to then we leave it up to chance, and what fills that void is often just as bad as what we turned from. True repentance turns to something specific. What is it that we turn to? We turn to Jesus Christ, we turn away from our sins and we turn to and trust in the blood of Jesus Christ, the price that was paid; and by faith, we trust that price.

The second step occurs when God forgives us. He forgives our sins and he saves our souls. The third step of this process is when he sends the Holy Spirit to seal our Salvation so it can never be taken away. Now the great thing about it is, the first step is the only one that we are responsible for. The second two, that's all God and He is faithful and just. Another great thing about steps two and three is that they happen at the same time and they happen quicker than it took me to explain them. You see, when we accept Jesus Christ as our savior, we get the indwelling of the Holy Spirit. The Holy Spirit comes into us, lives inside of us and most importantly, for the new convert, He seals us. Remember all the way back to your Sunday School days when you learned about Noah and the ark. God told Noah to pitch the ark within and without. You know what pitch does to a boat? It seals it. It keeps anything from getting in. Normally a boat is just pitched on the outside. You pitch a boat on the outside because you don't want the water coming in. When you pitch on the inside, you are trying to keep what is on the inside from getting out. Noah's ark was a picture of our salvation and when we are pitched on the inside and we are pitched on the outside, not only can nothing get into our salvation; nothing can get out of our salvation. We are sealed by the power of the Holy Ghost. The infinite power that created this universe seals us, and you cannot be unsaved.

I heard a story the other day about a singer, a Christian singer who said, "I have decided that I am not saved anymore." Well, guess what? You never were saved because you can't decide to be unsaved. What God has placed in the Son's hands, nothing can take out of his hands; nothing can remove it. No man can remove that. You say, "Well, what about me? I can remove myself." Well, aren't you a man? Nothing in mankind can take you away from God and God will not reject you. The same power that saved you is the power that keeps you. Think about this, the reason you can be saved is because of what took place on the cross. What took place on the cross is a greater good than any bad that you ever did in your life. It is a greater, more powerful thing than any bad that you ever will do in your life. There is no sin that we can do that is more evil than the good that Jesus Christ did on the cross, we are sealed. Remember, the only command for Christians regarding the Holy Spirit, other then don't quench the Holy Spirit, is to be filled by the Holy Spirit. What does that mean? It doesn't mean that we get more of the Holy Spirit; it means that the Holy Spirit gets more of us. We allow the Holy Spirit to have more control over us, more power over us.

When those three things, confession, salvation, & sealing happen, we will have conversion. Without those three steps, there can't be a conversion, but like I said, the only step that relies upon you is that first step. To be faithful and just, we trust that God will do His part...he is faithful and just to forgive us our sins. So the question isn't whether or not God will hold up his end of the bargain, whether or not he will hold up his end of the deal; the question is, will you confess? Will you confess your sins? 2 Corinthians 5:17 says, ***"Therefore if any man be in Christ, he is a new creature: old things are passed away; behold, all things are become new."*** When we confess our sins to God, He cleanses us and gives us the power to move beyond those sins; He gives us the power to move into a better life because of the Holy Spirit.

When you sin you are choosing something that is less than what God wanted for you. God has a perfect plan for you and when you sin, you are choosing something other than that perfect plan. Every time you sin, you are choosing something less. Now I know Satan makes it look like it is something better, but it is always something less than what God intended for you. That's why one of your jobs as a Christian is to tell people about sin. It is our job to tell people when they are doing something that is sinful, because want them to have the best life possible. We are not judging, we are simply pointing out to them that God has already judged sin. God has already shown that sin to be lacking and we want better for them, and better for them is not found in sin; better for them is found in the plan that God has for their life, and that is why we tell people. That is why we tell people what the Bible says they should not be doing, about lifestyles that go contrary to the word of God. It is not because we hate that person, it's not even because God hates that person; God loves that person and that is why God wants us to tell them. If your child was in danger... If your child was wandering into a place that was dangerous for them.... Maybe there is a pit bull loose and it is not a nice pit bull, it is a mean pit bull. We saw it and we are getting away from it when we see some little kids walking towards it and we say, you don't want to go that way because if you go that way, that dog is going to bite you, we want you to go this way. Do you think that child or their parents are going to say, "Who are you to judge my child? Who are you to tell my child where they can walk and where they can't walk? My child made a decision, they want to walk towards the dog, and they love dogs. They want to see the dog, who are you to tell my child that they can't go pet a rabid pit bull?" That is not what they are going to say, unless they are bad parents. But that is the mindset we expect from the world. When we tell someone that is living in a sinful state, when we tell the drunkard or we tell the homosexual or we tell anybody God has a better plan for you, we are not judging; we are simply telling them, that God has something better. Are you judging those children because they are walking towards the pit bull? No, you are warning them and telling them, there is a better way. That way is going to lead to destruction. Sin always leads to destruction, it doesn't matter how minor it seems, it doesn't matter how major it seems to us the results are the same: sin always leads to destruction. So when a Christian comes to you and tells you that there is sin in your life, you should be thanking that Christian, not condemning them.

1 John 2:1 says: ***"My little children, these things write I unto you, that ye sin not. And if any man sin, we have an advocate with the Father, Jesus Christ the righteous."***

With the Holy Spirit, it becomes difficult to sin. It becomes harder to sin once you accept Jesus Christ as your Saviour because now you've got the Holy Spirit inside of you to guide you. He is going to tell you things and he is going to whisper things, but as I mentioned before, we can quench the Holy Spirit. The more we resist, the quieter He gets. Eventually we get to a point where it doesn't even seem like He's even there anymore, but He is there. When we sin, and you notice it doesn't say, 'if' we sin, but when we sin, when we step off God's plan to take a path that is less, maybe we step into fornication or we step into drunkenness or we tell a lie, whatever it may be. No matter how big and no matter how little it seems, when we step off that perfect path, we have that same advocate that died for us on the cross, but now He is not dying for us as a Saviour, now He is standing as an advocate before the Father. You see, Satan watches and when you stumble, when you sin, Satan is the one who says, "Look God, did you see what Patti did? That's one of yours." Jesus steps in quickly and says, "I am her advocate. She did something wrong, she came to me, she has asked for forgiveness. That is taken care of, it's gone." We have an advocate that stands before God the Father, and that is Jesus Christ. So when we do sin, we go back to him again, same way. It has got to be heartfelt. Our confession cannot be, "Oh, got drunk today, I am going to get drunk next week, but I am going to go ahead and confess it today, then I will be done and I will be good until next week, then I will confess it again next week." That is not a true confession. A true confession is, "I am not going to do this again. I am not going to allow this to happen again." With that Holy Spirit inside of us it becomes more difficult to sin. Have you ever experienced that? As you get closer to God, things that used to feel comfortable to you, suddenly feel revolting to you? I have done that with movies that I had seen as a teenager. In my mind, I am thinking, "man that was a great movie." Then it comes on Netflix and 20 seconds in and I am like, "This is filth, this is garbage, I can't watch this." It is because as we draw closer to God, we begin to see things like God; we start to experience things like God and sin that didn't offend us before, and now starts to be offensive to us and we don't want to be around it anymore.

There was a gentleman that I was witnessing to for quite a while and he finally accepted Christ as his Saviour one Sunday following a Church Service. He accepted Christ as his Saviour, but he had a problem with alcohol and the next weekend I get a call on Saturday morning and he is crying. I asked, "What's wrong?" He said, "I got drunk last night." I said, "Well you shouldn't have done that." He replied "I did, I got drunk and now I don't think I am saved." I asked, "Well, why would getting drunk make you think that you are not still saved?" He answered, "Because if I was saved I wouldn't have gotten drunk." I said, "Well, didn't you get drunk last weekend?" He answered, "Yes." I asked, "Why didn't you call me last Saturday?" He said, "Well it didn't bother me then." I happily assured him, "You getting drunk doesn't prove you're not saved, but the fact that you woke up regretting it indicates that something has changed in you." He gave me his story; he said, "I was some place I should not have been. I got there and I knew it, I could hear it in my head saying, 'you are not supposed to be here, you are not supposed to be here.'" I said, "That is the Holy Spirit, the Holy Spirit is telling you, you are not supposed to be here, this is not where you are supposed to be. He said, "But I told myself it was okay that I can be here, I just won't drink anything. And I did good for a while, when people kept offering me something, I kept saying, 'No, no, no, I am not drinking.' And pretty soon someone puts a bottle into my hand and I think well I will just hold it and that little voice said, 'You shouldn't even be touching it, you shouldn't even be around it.' I will just hold it, it's okay, I am not going to drink it, I am just going to hold it and pretty soon I took a sip. It's okay, it's just a sip, it okay, it won't bother me, I can control this. Then a second bottle, then a third bottle, then I woke up this morning crying because I had failed God." Everything he described is all evidence that he is saved, because now even though he is still sinning, it just got a lot harder. It got a lot harder to sin and now he is feeling guilty for his sin. We have an advocate. When we wake up on those Saturday mornings, we have an advocate we can go to. You don't have to call me and confess, you can go right to the Father. Through the power of Jesus Christ your advocate, you can go right to the Father and say "I'm sorry, I'm sorry." The same power that saves you is the same power that can forgive you again.

The last part of John 1:9 says: *"...and to cleanse us from all unrighteousness."* When you get a wound, you don't just bandage it up, you clean it out first and He cleans us when we sin. He doesn't just leave us the way we were, He makes us a new creature and he cleans us out, he makes us clean again. He cleans our souls, He takes out all the unrighteousness and then He places in us hope for that new life. That hope for his second coming, that life that will satisfy us, that life that will finally be pleasing before God; he plants that inside of us. He gives us the ability and the will to be able to do those things. He gives us the power to get good. Did you love my English there? With Jesus, we can all get good. You see, the world wants us to see it the other way around. My Grandpa used to call that, getting the cart before the horse. They want to do it the other way around and get good before they get God. You will talk to people and invite them to church and they will say, "Oh, I am not really a church person, but I will go someday. First I want to quit smoking and I want to quit cursing and I want to live my life and I want to do this or that and then I will go to church. Then maybe I will get good enough to where I can go to church. Maybe I can get good enough to go before God. If I went before God now or if I go to church now, the building would fall in on me." Did you know that none of us are good enough to stand before God? If we were good enough, or could make ourselves good enough, for God we wouldn't need Jesus. None of us are good enough for God. None of us are worthy to stand in his presence, but with Jesus Christ and his righteousness, not only can we stand in His presence, but also we can walk boldly into His throne room. We have the right afforded to us as children of the King now. The children of the King don't have to wait in line. The children of the King get to bypass the line and walk boldly into the presence of their Father. Why? Because we are now His child and the child always has access to the Father. You see, when we try to get good before we get God, that puts the cart before the horse and what that means through Bible terms is, we are trying to save ourselves through our works. We are not saved by our works; we are not saved by our goodness because we can't be good enough. We are only saved through the power of Jesus Christ. We are only saved by the price that he paid on the cross. The one that could do no sin but took all of our sins upon Him. That is how we are saved. This is the message we need to share with the world. The world doesn't like it because when you start peeling back and you start working on those wounds, it hurts and it causes pain and the world doesn't like the pain.

The bible tells us in Romans 3:23 that we have all sinned. We have all sinned and we all come in short of God's plan for us. We all come short of what God wanted for us. We have come short of His glory, every one of us. The Bible tells us in Romans 6:23 that *"the wages of sin is death."* This is why we have to tell the world, because the world is condemned to death. They are walking towards the rabid pit bull and we have the information to save them. We need to tell them to turn around. We have to tell the world to turn around before it is too late. If you have never accepted Jesus Christ as your Saviour, you are walking towards something that is even bigger and meaner than a rapid pit bull; you are walking towards the fires of hell and it will destroy you. It doesn't matter how little you think your sin is, it will destroy you. It doesn't matter how hidden you think your sin is, it will destroy you. It doesn't matter how personal you think your sin is, it will destroy you. The wages of sin is death; not might be death, is death.

When the Bible talks about death, it talks about death in two senses. It talks about physical death and it talks about spiritual death. Physical death, we understand. We would be hard-pressed to find anybody that has not been touched personally by physical death. Whether it was a parent, a spouses, a child or a friend we have all been touched by physical death. But there is a greater death than physical death, and that is spiritual death. That is when we spend our eternity separated from God. We spend our eternity separated from Him in hell because we chose our way instead of His way. We earn what we deserve, our wages, and the wages of sin is death. Thankfully that same verse that says, *"...the wages of sin is death,"* continues to say, *"but the gift of God is eternal life through Jesus Christ our Lord."* Think about that for a minute. Wages, what we have earned, what we deserve, what we should have, that is death, but the gift, a gift is something that we don't earn. A gift is something that we don't even deserve. A gift is something that is given to us out of love. The gift of God is eternal life. Don't you love that? You know what I really love about that? That verse, the more I study that verse, the bigger that verse gets because I used to think, "Oh, God gives us the opposite, the opposite of death which is life." You know what? Life technically isn't the opposite of death. Death is the absence of life; it is different. We won't get into all that here, but He doesn't just give us life, He gives us eternal life. So even if death and life were opposite of each other and He goes beyond that, He doesn't just give us life, He gives us eternal life. Eternal life, we can't even comprehend. We try to, but we understand life as what we experience in this world, but that isn't the life that He is talking about. He is not talking about this existence forever because I will be honest with you, I will still choose this over hell, but I don't want to live like this the rest of my life. I mean, I am fat and happy, but I don't want to be fat and happy for all of eternity, I want to get out of this shell. I want to get beyond this, I want to get out of this world, I want to get beyond this world, I want to get beyond the confines of this world, I want to get beyond the confines of my small mind, I want to get outside of that and that is what He offers us. He offers us a heaven that, when the writers of the Bible try to tell us about it, there weren't even words to describe it. John did his very best in the Book of Revelation.

Sometimes people get offended when I say, "You are

not worthy of God, you are not worthy to stand in His presence." People, they bristle up, but I love that. Just let me finish this thought before you start judging me here. I love the fact that I am not worthy for God, not that I revel in my sin, but because being a sinner, being not worthy, He loves me so much, and He is still willing to save me. If I was worthy of it, where's the love? He loves me, in spite of me. If we made our lists earlier and wrote all of our sins down and passed them out to other people without our names on it and asked, "Is this a loving person, is this somebody that you could love?" most of us would look at it and say, "That is not somebody I want to love." But this is somebody that God loves. This is somebody that Jesus Christ died for because He loved them so much. See, we are not very loveable, and yet God loves us more than anything and He has done everything, including sacrificing His Son, to make sure that you have a place in heaven. What you have to do is you have to confess. If you have never accepted Jesus Christ as your Saviour, will you confess today? Will you accept Jesus Christ today?

Assuming that you have accepted Jesus Christ as your Saviour, I want to look a little deeper into the duration of your salvation. I Thessalonians 5:23-24 tells us: ***"And the very God of peace sanctify you wholly; and I pray God your whole spirit and soul and body be preserved blameless unto the coming of our Lord Jesus Christ. Faithful is He that calleth you, who also will do it."***

There's a lot of false teachings out there that tell us that we can obtain salvation and lose salvation often almost simultaneously. That every time we sin we separate ourselves from God and we lose our place in Heaven. That's not what the Bible says. The man-made religions of the world teach that it is up to us to maintain and to hold on to our salvation. But the verses in 1 Thessalonians that we just read say, *"Your whole spirit and soul be preserved blameless unto the coming of the Lord Jesus Christ."* Verse number 24, it says, *"Faithful is He that calleth you, who also will do it."* One of the great things about our salvation is that God did all the work. We are saved 100% by His grace. We don't deserve salvation. We don't deserve God's blessings upon us. We receive salvation completely by the grace of God. Because if it was up to us to earn salvation we would never be able to earn it. We'd never be able to do enough good. So why is it that we can comprehend the concept that it is up to God to save us, but think it's up to us to maintain our salvation? We are no more equipped to maintain our salvation than we are to achieve our salvation in the first place. God will do it. God maintains it. If it was up to us, none of us would make it to Heaven because none of us could maintain our salvation perfectly. We couldn't do it.

We all understand- at least I hope you understand, that you were created on purpose, that God has a special purpose for you. You have a point of service. There is a place where God expects you to serve Him. There is a place where God has preordained and planned to put you, a place where you will thrive there more than you will thrive anywhere else. That's your point of service. And I pray to God that you will find that point because God created you on purpose, for a purpose. But Satan also has a purpose for you. When you were created by God, Satan had a purpose for you. His purpose wasn't to control you. His purpose wasn't to make you stumble. His purpose wasn't to indwell you and take you over and steal your soul. His purpose wasn't any of those things. He had one purpose for you, and that was to destroy you. He wants you destroyed. He doesn't want you serving him. He wants you destroyed. Never forget that. He doesn't want you to worship him. He wants you destroyed. How does he destroy you? By keeping you from accepting Jesus Christ, by distracting you with the things of this world, by distracting you with the things of your mind, by distracting you with the lust of your flesh, by distracting you away from the message of Jesus Christ and keeping you out of Heaven, by never allowing you to be saved in the first place, and by keeping you distracted away from Jesus and tempted in other directions. But once you're saved Satan can't destroy you. Your soul cannot be destroyed once you've been saved.

But Satan still has another purpose for you. Once you've accepted Christ as your Saviour, Satan doesn't give up on you. He can't steal your soul. He can't destroy your soul. He can't have you join him when he is cast into Hell. He can't do any of those things but he can make you an ineffective Christian. How does he do that? Through doubt. If he can get you to doubt for a moment that you're saved then he's won you for that moment. As I mentioned above, we all have an ordained point of service and there is great variety in how that service manifests itself. But there's one thing that all of us, no matter where we serve, have in common. We have that commission to go and to tell the world about Jesus Christ. It doesn't matter where you serve, whether you stand in the pulpit, work in the sound booth, collect up the offering, or you teach Sunday school, your service boils down to one basic purpose and that's to go and to tell people about Jesus Christ. That's our job as Christians. If Satan can get you to doubt your salvation, he can get you to stop going and stop telling. How can you go and tell somebody about something that you're not really sure you believe yourself?

I want to make sure we are clear on this. The man-made religions of this world are pushing this false teaching. According to them you can be saved and then unsaved, and then resaved again and unsaved again. It's a continual process. So that when they die, they die without any hope and the family stands around and wonders, "Well I wonder if he's in Heaven or not, today." I'm going to make it easy for you. For those of you that outlive me, when I die, you don't have to wonder about where I am.

I'll tell you where I'm going to be because when I close my eyes here, I'm going to be in the presence of my Lord. That's where I'm opening up my eyes. You don't have to wonder, you don't have to hope I made it because I'll be honest with you, if it was up to me to make it, I wouldn't make it. But I'll be in Heaven by the Grace of God and by nothing else. I will be maintained by the Grace of God and nothing else.

I think part of the confusion is caused by people who claim to be Christians but never truly repented and accepted Christ as their Saviour. They claim to be Christian but their lives say something very different. Anybody can say anything. Saying that you're a believer doesn't make you a believer any more than changing my nickname to "Skinny" is going to make me thin. The Bible talks extensively about these fake believers. Matthew describes them as wolves in sheep's clothing and tares among the wheat. A tare among the wheat looks a lot like the wheat but it's not wheat. It never produces the grain. It never produces anything profitable. Those are the people that say they're believers and that show up on Sunday mornings, but you never see anything profitable coming out of their life. There's never any heavenly fruit coming out of their life. They look right, they sound right, you can't really tell them one from the other except one produces and one doesn't produce. That's where you'll see the difference. They're the tares among the wheat. Peter calls them *"wells without water."* I love that description. They look like a well, they're dug like a well, everything about them screams well but when you go and you try and get any moisture out of them, any water out of them, they're dry. They're empty.

These aren't people that were saved and then aren't saved anymore. These are people who were never saved in the first place. Ephesians 2:8 says: ***"For by grace are ye saved through faith; and that not of yourselves: it is the gift of God: Not of works, lest any man should boast."***

Oftentimes these tares among the wheat or these dry wells, these are people who are trying to earn their place in Heaven. They figure if they can come and do their penance, show up for church on Sunday morning, or put some money in the offering plate they can work their way into heaven. We are not saved by works; we are saved by grace. There's nothing we can do to earn ourselves into heaven. If we could earn our way into heaven then what was the point of Jesus dying on the cross? We could just all be good and get into heaven. But it doesn't work that way. Romans 11:6 *"And if by grace, then is it no more of works: otherwise grace is no more grace. But if it be of works, then is it no more grace: otherwise work is no more work."*

Look at the last part of that verse again, *"...otherwise grace is no more grace."* When we add anything to grace, grace ceases to exist and we end up with what I call, "salvation plus". If I had a pitcher of water, nice, cool, clear water- and I asked, "Who would like some of this cool, clear, water?" and I started pouring it in the glass real slow- can you see the water? Can you see it going in the glass? Going in nice and slow and gurgling in? How many of you are getting thirsty right now? Who would like some of this pure water? But before you drink it I put a couple drops of this rat poison in the glass. Now, who wants some? Nobody. Why? Because it's not water anymore, is it? Now it's something deadly. And when we take anything, it doesn't matter how small it is, it doesn't matter how unimportant it seems, when we take anything and we add it to grace, it's not grace anymore. It's something else and whatever that other thing is, it cannot save us. Only grace can save us. The entire act of salvation from beginning to end relies upon grace and nothing else. Nothing more, nothing less. Anything added always destroys the grace.

Our salvation is also secured because of the work of Christ. John 10:28 *"And I give unto them eternal life; and they shall never perish, nether shall any man pluck them out of my hand."*

Let me ask you a question. How long is eternal life? Is eternal life just until you mess up? That's not eternal life, is it? If you went to the store, the guy says, "I've got the best tires for your truck right here. These tires will never go flat. They cost a little bit more but they'll never go flat, they'll never wear out. These are the perfect tires," you'd probably buy those tires. Then a week later you run over a nail and you get a flat. And when you return to the store they tell you that nail punctures aren't covered in the guarantee. That's not the same, is it? The salesman was being deceitful. And to say that our salvation is eternal until we mess up, until we sin again, that's being deceitful. When Jesus says you are saved eternally, do you know what He means? He means that you are saved eternally.

Our salvation is also secured because of the work of the Father. John 10:29 *"My Father which gave them me, is greater than all; and no man is able to pluck them out of my Father's hand."*

We're not just secure by the work of Jesus, we're also secure by the work of the Father. The Son and the Father working together.

Our salvation is also secured because of the work of the Holy Spirit. John 14:16 says: *"And I will pray the Father, and He shall give you another Comforter, that He may abide with you forever."*

How long does the Holy Spirit abide with us? Until

we mess up? No. Forever. We're also secured not just by the Son, not just by the Father, but by the power of the Holy Spirit. All 3 persons of God are active and working to secure your salvation. It's not about us, it's about Them.

One of my favorite passages in the Bible is in Ephesians chapter 1, verse 13 *"In whom ye also trusted, after that ye heard the word of truth, the gospel of your salvation: in whom also after that ye believed, ye were sealed with that holy Spirit of promise, which is the earnest of our inheritance until the redemption of the purchased possession, unto the praise of His glory."*

This passage is talking about the contract that God signed with the blood of Jesus Christ when we were saved. At that contract there was some earnest given. That earnest is the Holy Spirit. To fully understand the magnitude of these verses we have to understand what an earnest is. Normally we see earnest when contracts are signed. In short, earnest is something that is given to ensure the completion of a contract. I'll make a very simple picture of earnest here for you. Let's say I'm going to go and buy a house. Laura's going to sell me a house that costs $100,000. The problem is I don't have $100,000 today, but I will have it next week. All I have today is $10,000. So I'll tell her, "This is what I'll do, I'm going to give you some earnest money. I don't have $100,000, but I've got $10,000. If I give you $10,000 of earnest money will you hold it until next week when I promise to give you the other $90,000?" And she's going to say yes, you know why? Because 1 of 2 things happens next week. Either I come back and I complete

115

the transaction, or I don't and she keeps the $10,000 worth of earnest money. You see, if the transaction is not completed as promised, the earnest is forfeited. Now think through this with me. The Holy Spirit is the earnest of our salvation. What does that mean? He's our down payment. He's the guarantee. If God does not maintain our salvation, if God fails to keep us until that final day, do you know what God loses? The Holy Spirit. That is not going to happen because God will fulfil His contract. He's placed Himself, His Holy Spirit on the block saying, "This is how serious I am about you. This is how much I love you. This is how much I promise to maintain you. I am going to give Myself as earnest and if I don't come through at the end then you get to keep It." That's how serious He is about maintaining our salvation.

So where does the confusion come from? Confusion generally comes from 1 of 2 places. It's either satanic/demonic in influence, or in other words they're purposely feeding confusion into the world, or there's a bigger source of confusion. Confusion comes from our own minds. Confusion comes from our own lack of understanding. Confusion comes from our laziness with the handling of the Scripture. Confusion comes from us failing to rightly divide the Word of God.

I want you to look at four verses that are commonly used by groups who teach the false doctrine that we can lose our salvation. In other words, we can be damned after we're saved and we can be cast into Hell after we're saved.

1 Corinthians 11:29 *"For he that eatheth and*

drinketh unworthily, eateth and drinketh damnation to himself, not discerning the Lord's body."

Romans 14:23 *"And he that doubteth is damned if he eat, because he eateth not of faith: for whatsoever is not of faith is sin."*

Romans 13:2 *"Whosoever therefore resisteth the power, resisteth the ordinance of God: and they that resist shall receive to themselves damnation."*

1 Timothy 5:12 *"Having damnation, because they have cast off their first faith."*

There are a few problems with trying to twist these verses to mean something they don't. First, these verses contradict other verses in the Bible and when you come to verses in the Bible that seem to contradict each other, understand, you're interpreting one of those verses incorrectly. It behooves us to dig deeper and find out why we are understanding it this way. Why does the Bible one place say that we're saved forever, another one say if you do this, you're damned? That doesn't sound right, does it? That sounds like a conflict. Groups that are willing to say that you can lose your salvation are willing to cling to these verses and ignore the other verses that God gave us that tell us that we're saved eternally, that tell us that it's God's job to maintain our salvation, not ours.

Secondly, if you go back to the original Greek text, the word used for damnation in every one of these verses is the word, *"Krima."* Krima always refers to an earthly damnation, a physical damnation. It's never

117

referring to a spiritual damnation. Those are bad things. And they're going to cause huge problems. I Corinthians 11:29 was talking about the Lord's Supper. It's talking about taking the Lord's Supper unworthily, eating when you're not supposed to. It will not take your salvation away from you but it will cause you huge problems on this earth, in the physical realm.

The word that's used for a spiritual damnation is *"Anathema."* That word refers to damnation on a spiritual level, in other words, a casting into Hell. So we have to understand that when things contradict, there's a reason why they're contradicting. It's because we're not understanding what we're reading. Pray for the Holy Spirit to sort those things out for you and dig a little deeper when you come to those things.

Matthew 7:21 is another the passage that's used to teach confusion; it says: ***"Not everyone that saith unto me, 'Lord, Lord,' shall enter into the kingdom of heaven; but he that doeth the will of my Father which is in heaven. Many will say to me in that day, 'Lord, Lord, have we not prophesied in thy name? And in thy name have we not cast out devils? And in thy name done many wonderful works? And then I will profess unto them, 'I never knew you: depart from me, ye that work iniquity."***

Now at first glance, this sounds like believers who are proclaiming Jesus, who are casting out devils, who are preaching in His name and then when they get to Heaven, somehow, somewhere along the way, they've lost their salvation, they've been cast out. Until you get to that last part where Jesus says, ***"I never knew you."***

You see, if they had been Christians that lost their salvation, He couldn't say, "I never knew you." He'd have to say, "I don't know you anymore," or "I used to know you but you turned away from Me." To say, "I never knew you," means that they were never saved. They may have proclaimed it. The really startling part for me in this is, this isn't talking about your average "Christian." This is talking about religious leaders that have stood in pulpits and proclaimed the name of God but they've never received the Salvation of Jesus Christ. We're not saved by talking about Jesus. We're not saved by proclaiming Jesus. We're saved by Grace through faith, receiving the gift of salvation. You can talk till you're blue in the face but it won't save you.

Another verse sometimes misused is 1 John 2:19. It says: *"They went out from us, but they were not of us; for if they had been of us, they would no doubt have continued with us: but they went out, that they might be made manifest that they were not all of us."*

Again, this isn't talking about people that have lost their salvation. These are people who were with the disciples and then left the disciples. But they are clearly talking about people who were never Christians. *"They were not of us."*

Some of you reading this are like the people that were described in these passages. Some of you have been clinging to something other than Jesus Christ for your salvation. Some of you have been clinging to an act, or some of you have been clinging to a religion, or some of you have been clinging to work to get you into Heaven, and you're going to stand before Christ one day and He is going to proclaim that, *"I never knew you."*

Sometimes when I am driving I start to think about things other than my destination. When I finally snap out of it I realize I missed my turn or I have gone way past my destination. Has that ever happened to you? You know where you're supposed to be going but, for whatever reason, you're going in the wrong direction. You're going the wrong way. When I discover that I'm going to the wrong place, I have a choice I need to make. I can either continue on the path that I'm on, the path that's not going to get me any closer to where I need to be. Or I can turn around and I can go to where I'm supposed to be going. Now driving is a little different than our spirituality because I can turn around on the highway and nobody knows that I made a mistake. It's hard for some people to admit they have been going the wrong way on their Spiritual journey because they lived in church, and they were raised in church, and they've been coming to church for so long that to finally make the admission that, "I've been going about this wrong but I never got it in my heart," is embarrassing. It can be embarrassing to finally come to that point and say, "You know what, if I don't do something, I'm going to die and I'm going to go to Hell." You know the path that you're on and you're hoping that things will get better, but things aren't going to get better until you stop and you turn back to Jesus Christ; until you turn and accept what He did for you on the cross. Nothing else you're doing is going to get you to where you need to go.

I really, really pray that none of you would let the

embarrassment of admitting that you made a mistake, admitting that you were going in the wrong direction, admitting that you were trusting in the wrong thing- I pray that none of you would be so short-sighted that you would allow that embarrassment to embarrass you right into Hell. Show wisdom. Show strength. And turn to Jesus Christ. Many of you have accepted Christ as your Saviour, many of you haven't accepted Christ as your Saviour. I pray that today will be the day of your salvation.

Let's Go Deeper

1. What sins are you holding onto that need to be turned over to God today?

2. What are the three steps of conversion?

3. Which of those three steps relies upon you?

4. What area of your life has the Holy Spirit been working on?

5. Have you accepted Christ as your Saviour? If not, will you prayerfully consider doing that now?

6. Write I John 1:9 in the space below and make plans to memorize it this week.

For Pastors

When was the last time you led someone to the Lord? When was the last time you taught someone else to lead someone to the Lord? Soul winning Pastors lead soul winning churches. This lesson will lead those who are not born again or confused about their eternity to come forward during an altar call. I highly encourage you to have an altar call or something similar. For a few years I led services at the local jail. At each service we saw men giving their lives to Christ. Another Pastor came to me because He was concerned that he was not seeing any souls saved during his service, so I agreed to sit in one of his services and offer a critique. The service was wonderful, very well researched, passionate, and obviously well prayed over. But at the end he just dismissed the men; no altar call, no request for decisions to be made, nothing. This Pastor was setting a great table, but never inviting anyone to eat. He was not comfortable with an altar call but decided to give it a try. Guess what happened? He began seeing souls saved and lives transformed! Try an altar call at the end of this message and see what happens. Never set the table without inviting people to eat. Have your soul winners ready and reap the harvest!

Now that you've read the book, join me on my blog!

www.JayMcCaig.com

Made in the USA
Middletown, DE
24 June 2021